Agora Paperback Editions

GENERAL EDITOR: ALLAN BLOOM

Politics and the Arts

Politics and the Arts

LETTER TO M. D'ALEMBERT ON THE THEATRE

By Jean-Jacques Rousseau

TRANSLATED WITH NOTES AND INTRODUCTION

by Allan Bloom

CORNELL UNIVERSITY PRESS

ITHACA, NEW YORK

First published, Agora Editions, 1960
First printing, Agora Paperback Editions,
Cornell Paperbacks, 1968

This edition is reprinted by arrangement
with The Free Press.

Printed in the United States of America

ISBN-13: 978-0-8014-9071-2 (pbk. : alk. paper)
Library of Congress Catalog Card Number 60-7094

Cornell University Press strives to use environmentally responsible suppliers
and materials to the fullest extent possible in the publishing of its books.
Such materials include vegetable-based, low-VOC inks and acid-free papers
that are recycled, totally chlorine-free, or partly composed of nonwood fibers.
For further information, visit our website at www.cornellpress.cornell.edu.

Paperback printing   20   19   18   17   16   15   14

J.-J. ROUSSEAU

Letter to M. d'Alembert
on the Theatre

J.-J. Rousseau, Citizen of Geneva

TO

M. d'Alembert, of the French Academy, The Royal Academy of Sciences of Paris, the Prussian Academy, the Royal Society of London, the Royal Academy of Literature of Sweden, and the Institute of Bologna;

On his article *Geneva* in the seventh volume of *l'Encyclopédie* and especially on the project of establishing a dramatic theatre in that city.

Di meliora piis, erroremque hostibus illum.[1]
Virg. *Georg.* III. 513

NOTE: The numbers refer to the Translator's Notes at the end of the book; the asterisks to Rousseau's own notes at the bottom of the page.

Translator's Preface

The present translation is an attempt to render the French text into English as literally as possible consistent with intelligibility. Elegance and power, characteristics belonging to the original, have been subordinated to accuracy, in the conviction that the book is carefully written and that, while the success of an attempt to imitate style is always dubious, the sense can be conveyed in a modest way. With such a work the reader should not be at the mercy of the translator's often erroneous conviction that he has understood it; the reader should have the materials for finding new meanings and for establishing connections not visible on the surface. To this end, an effort has been made to translate all the central words used in the original with the same English word throughout, even at the risk of some awkwardness; this has not always been possible, but it was the standard. Concerning some words, explanatory notes have been added. A few notes were also necessary to explain some difficulties in rendering or to translate and locate passages and works cited or referred to; but there is no attempt to explain Rousseau's deeper meaning, to trace sources to which he does not choose to refer, nor to point out alleged errors of reasoning or fact; the text stands on its own.

The Fuchs edition published by Droz, Geneva, 1948, was used as the basis of the translation; this is the text of the first edition published in 1758. All important changes made in later editions, up to the last one corrected by Rousseau himself, published in 1782, have been either included in the text or cited in notes. Two other important critical editions are those of Fontaine, published by Garnier, Paris, 1889, and of Brunel, published by Hachette, Paris, 1916.

I wish to express my gratitude to Messrs. Burton Feldman, Morris Parslow, Marvin Zetterbaum, and Hugues de Giorgis for their generous help in correcting the manuscript. Mr. Thomas McDonald deserves my thanks for going through the translation with his usual care and delicacy; he is responsible for none of the errors to be found in it but prevented many that would have been.

I am deeply indebted to the Committee on Legal and Political Philosophy of the Rockefeller Foundation for the grant which made it possible for me to undertake this work.

The substance of the introduction was first delivered as a lecture at Ohio State University in February, 1959, the occasion for which I owe thanks to Professors Harry V. Jaffa and Harvey C. Mansfield.

Allan Bloom
Chicago, March, 1959

Contents

* The table of contents for the body of the *Letter* is entirely by the translator. The original has no divisions into chapters and sections. The above
division is intended only to help the reader to get a unified view of the whole
and, although it attempts to follow the natural articulation of the work, it does
not pretend to be an authoritative key to Rousseau's organization.

Introduction

Any suggestion favoring censorship in the arts and sciences is most naturally viewed by us with suspicion as arising from the illiberal interest of party or sect. The arms of repression have so long been used only to bolster corrupt and decaying regimes or to institute tyrannical ones that the free development of the arts now appears to be a necessary condition, if not the core, of a republican way of life. It is hard to believe that during the greater part of recorded history disinterested, that is to say, philosophic, men were of the opinion that republics required the greatest self-imposed restraints whereas tyrannies and other decadent regimes could often afford the greatest individual liberties. They began from the presupposition that a free society governed by its members is in need of the most careful education in order that the citizens have the requisite virtues for ruling themselves and one another. Hence, all the elements of moral and intellectual training are a legitimate object of concern to the society as a whole, which should in principle be willing to sacrifice even very charming or respectable pursuits on the altar of its liberty, if they happen to conflict with that most valuable of possessions. In this perspective, all studies and forms of entertainment must justify themselves before the bar of public utility and prove that, if not positively salutary, they are at least not harmful to the order on which self-government is founded; no form of science or art can be assumed to be beneficial prior to examination, and the difficulty of judging such questions does not do away with the necessity for their consideration.

For the older writers, this form of political supervision of the arts is to be sharply distinguished from the arbitrary repression by

weak and frightened governments of anything they consider
threatening, contrary to all principles of justice and decency; nor
can it be identified with the ever renascent attempts to destroy the
freedom of citizens to speak their minds honestly concerning public affairs. Far rather it was understood to be the means by which
citizens able and willing to take a real and courageous interest in
public affairs could be formed. And, indeed, even those who proposed the most liberal policies concerning the arts and sciences
prior to the nineteenth century felt themselves obliged to argue
that the liberties they defended would in themselves lend to the
establishment and perpetuation of republican institutions and to
make distinctions between those which should be accepted and
those which should be banished. They did not differ from their
opponents about the principle of censorship; they only denied that
the limits proposed by the more severe were advantageous to self-
government.

We, on the contrary, tend to see in censorship only the instruments of tyranny and a threat to freedom; what was formerly the
concern of republics now appears to be only the interest of totali-
tarians. Democracy seems to need no defense, or, to put it otherwise, it is generally assumed that the progress of the arts must necessarily parallel that of civil society or that their unlimited freedom
insures the discovery and political dominance of the truth. Generally, such a position implies as its premise, often unexamined, the
idea of progress. If we do not accept this notion, if freedom is
always threatened and barbarism always possible, the whole question must be reopened; an attempt must be made to discuss in a
thoroughgoing manner the conditions of free government and to
find the principles by which the various pursuits which claim admission to a republic can be judged. All this must be done in order
to be able to distinguish between the really important elements of
our liberty and the pretenders which have gained credit by assimi-
lating themselves to the truly necessary and noble pursuits; the fate
of the most cherished rights should not be bound up with that of

a licence and self-indulgence incapable of resisting impartial examination. Such consideration is necessary not only for the legislator
but also for the artist, who can thereby reflect on his responsibilities
to civil society, a duty he can easily shirk when encouraged by an
ideology which persuades him that whatever he does will be for
the good of the whole.

Since the habit of reflection on these issues has disappeared, and
with it even the terms of the debate, we must, in order to remind
ourselves, return to the discussion as it existed prior to the emergence of the idea of progress as a fixed doctrine. One of the last
great voices raised in favor of censorship was Jean Jacques Rousseau, who presented a detailed account of the effects of the arts
on civil society. The occasion for his interest in this problem was
his quarrel with the Enlightenment, his break with those who believed that the cultivation of reason, the progress in the sciences
and the dissemination of the results of that knowledge, as well as
the taste for the fine arts, would make society ever more decent and
men ever happier. Since Descartes and Spinoza, all the pens of
philosophers had battled against the restrictions, political and religious, which hindered the free pursuit of their activities; and most
generous men had been persuaded to recognize the Republic of
Letters as a legitimate society of the wise established within the
boundaries of the existing regimes, a society at times at odds with
the rulers of the real republics, but one which by its lights would
gradually transform the others and lead them to a justice and a
glory surpassing those of the ancients. Philosophy would purge
men of prejudice and make their duties clear without the aid of
superstition; the fine arts would civilize them and remove their
barbarous rudeness, a vestige of earlier times; and the mechanical
arts would procure them a longer and more comfortable life.

This project reached its most definitive expression in Rousseau's
time with *l'Encyclopédie*, the major divisions of which correspond to the three parts of the project. *L'Encyclopédie* was the
life work of great and devoted men who offered up their talents to

the betterment of humanity and who risked their security in the struggle against fanatic opposition. All that was decent and fine seemed to be on their side, and they took for granted that their gifted contemporary would join them, as would all men of science and learning, in their attempt to present the whole of human intellectual achievement in a clear form for the public. But Rousseau decided to use his great eloquence to oppose them and to stand, alone, for virtue, the science of simple souls—virtue, whose place he could not find in any of the parts of *l'Encyclopédie* and whose interests, in his view, ran counter to those of the Encyclopedists. Rousseau, who should have been the heir of his illustrious predecessors, willingly disinherited himself and perversely and incomprehensibly chose Rome, Sparta, and primitivism over the polished charm of modernity. He appears to have substituted for science a sentimental longing for an irretrievable but heroic past, a past degraded and debunked by the criticisms of reason; thus we have come to call him the father of romanticism.

To understand the motives behind Rousseau's unaccountable rejection of his birthright we must look to the particular reasons he himself adduces for it in his writings; a general dissatisfaction with modernity cannot account for it, nor can it be reduced to a mere expression of Rousseau's own incapacity to live in this later age. One of the most revealing documents we possess in this respect is his *Letter to d'Alembert on the Theatre*. Rousseau, the most personal of philosophers, had a way of endowing the incidents of his life with the most general significance, of making them mere reverberations of cosmic conflicts. He tried to represent in his person the deepest problems of humanity. The *Letter to d'Alembert* is a good illustration of this rule; it can be, and has often been, interpreted as another example of Rousseau's vanity, spitefulness, and madness; all of this may very well be true, but it is not the whole truth. Careful study of this neglected work gives evidence of the clear and easily defensible character of the reasoning which led him to condemn the theatre as a form of entertainment. The present translation is dedicated to its revival.

The particular circumstances which provided the occasion for this book—which constituted his definitive break with the Encyclopedists—are reminiscent of a drama whose particular events are all meant to epitomize general issues; it is like a morality play, entitled "The Spirit of the Enlightenment against the Spirit of Republican Virtue." The *dramatis personae* are Rousseau, the protagonist; d'Alembert, the editor of *l'Encyclopédie* and the author of its plan; and behind him, unmentioned but nevertheless the key figure, the genius of the Enlightenment incarnate, Voltaire. The circumstances were, briefly, the following: Voltaire, in his exile, had gone to live on the outskirts of Geneva in the year 1755. Geneva, the birthplace of Rousseau and the modern image of the antique *polis* for him, was a republic governed by its citizens; it was the city of Calvin and was noted for a severe civic code that included sumptuary laws and a ban on the theatre. A city so near France could not help being influenced by its atmosphere and a large body of Genevans wanted to share in the sophisticated marvels of the French theatre; they were opposed by the clergy. Voltaire, who represented the theatre, who hoped to civilize and to instruct with it, and who loved to see and act in plays, brought a new impetus to the dispute; he was bored without a theatre and set himself up in opposition to the interdiction, single-handedly undertaking to overturn Geneva's laws and take advantage of the unlawful craving for the theatre to be found in many Genevans, even among the clergy. One weapon to be used in the struggle was *l'Encyclopédie* with its enormous influence in affecting opinion. An article on Geneva was to appear in 1757, and Voltaire persuaded d'Alembert, who was to write it, to insert a passage (which Rousseau insists Voltaire himself wrote) in an otherwise laudatory presentation suggesting that Geneva should have a theatre, a theatre governed by stern laws so that the Genevans could refine their taste and combine the civility of the Athenians with the virtues of the Spartans. At this, in early 1758, Rousseau entered the fray, indignant that the authority of the sciences should be used to gratify the passions of an individual to what he tried to demonstrate was the detriment of Geneva. To him this represented what Enlightenment could easily become. He used his powerful rhetoric, a rhetoric that has perhaps never been equaled in its capacity to move the hearts of contemporaries and to express their unavowed wishes, to defeat Voltaire, and in so doing Rousseau presented as complete a treatment of the arts in relation to politics as has ever been produced. Such a treatment requires an analysis of the whole character of political life: hence the *Letter to d'Alembert* is a comprehensive theoretical work—one that looks at civil society from what might be the most revealing viewpoint, that of its relation to the works of the mind.

As I have said, the *Letter to d'Alembert* is a work of rhetoric, a public letter designed to have a persuasive effect on a particular audience. It is directed to this audience; the arguments used are appropriate to it; and the things chosen to be said or left out of consideration, as well as the style, depend on its special character. Rhetoric, by its very nature, implies that simple reason does not suffice for persuasion, that there is an element of unreason and passion which is an essential part of the understanding of man; the very form indicates a problem which supplements our understanding of the subject matter contained within it. Rousseau's audience is the many, and this means the many who are the subjects of civil society. He indicates that the dimension of politics is other than that of science or philosophy, and he repeats again and again that the considerations he raises and the way in which he argues them are limited by those to whom he speaks. Hence much that is found elsewhere in his thought is not to be found in the *Letter to d'Alembert*. He identifies himself with the many, and whatever in him may transcend their limits can only be alluded to here; the rest of himself is irrelevant and perhaps noxious to civil society.

Only he who believes in a natural harmony between civil society and the few best individuals can afford to forget this problem. This helps to account for the paradoxical tone of Rousseau's thought as a whole; it is not a result of his own complications but of those of human life itself, of which he is only a most revealing reflection due to his peculiar sensitivity to things in their breadth and depth. Politics must be a separate study because of the reasons implied in the fact that rhetoric must be used in it; if it were to be studied from the point of view of the whole or of what is simply desirable for the best man, it would lose its outlines. So it is not as "le pauvre Jean-Jacques" that he addresses himself to the problem of a theatre in Geneva but as "J.-J. Rousseau, Citizen of Geneva." Out of philanthropy he identifies himself with his fellows and makes himself hardly distinguishable from them. He underlines this by addressing d'Alembert as a member of six learned societies, drawing the sharpest contrast between his unadorned citizenship and d'Alembert's titles of science. He wishes to make it understood that articles like the one on Geneva are not really philosophic, that they only pretend to be, that they are trying to persuade; but, because their authors do not seriously consider the difference between disinterested search for truth and the necessary prejudices and special interests of political life, their science not only turns into propaganda but also damages the real interests of their nations; society can never be fully rational, and the attempt to make it so perverts science and corrupts society. Man in society is governed by habits, and reason is more likely to provide him with arguments for self-indulgence than with incentive to do his duty. The practice of the arts, which can ennoble some, creates an atmosphere which encourages the many who are not artists to pursue mere pleasure. There is a disproportion between science understood by itself and human happiness; human happiness is Rousseau's choice, at least here. It is something different to speak as a philosopher and as a citizen.

Rousseau, who attacks writers and discourages science, must explain why he writes and why he himself is so avid for learning that he has devoted his life to it. He cannot deny that there are rare men of special talents; nor, when defending a state like Geneva, can he contend that savagery is sufficient. When he appears in the guise of a citizen, he gives it to be understood that the function of his talents is to defend society against false theories and the improper use of reason. Men like Socrates, Newton, and Bacon were great because they were motivated by love of mankind and were protectors of virtue. They were reticent in their manner of speech not because of fear of their contemporaries, as d'Alembert suggests in the Preliminary Discourse to *l'Encyclopédie,* but out of duty to them. So Rousseau presents his science as not of value in itself but only insofar as it fulfils this clear purpose. He was forced to write by d'Alembert; he would have preferred to remain silent. But his duty to his country compels him to take up his pen and sacrifice his leisure; he must also endanger his reputation. Further, he is an example of a man to whom principle means more than propriety or politeness; the rules of mutual self-indulgence current among literary men cannot prevent him from hearing the call of virtue. By this posture, he again distinguishes himself from his contemporaries and sets the example for a healthy morality unaffected by the conventions of polite society. He is dying, and his last efforts are given to his country in a time of need. Corresponding to this description is the atmosphere of sentiment which Rousseau attempts to create by his Preface. He stimulates the passion of beneficence, of sympathy for one's fellow creatures. In his correction of Hobbes and the whole tradition depending on him, Rousseau argues that, if passion is the root of sociality, self-love is not the passion sufficient to bind society together nor on which to base men's duties to one another; another passion, not derivative from self-love, exists, and it is beneficence. The progress of society and science succeeds in dimming its lights, and vanity takes its place. But the health of society depends on fanning the embers of beneficence; it is the only truly social passion, and Rousseau tries to speak to it, or, as he would say, to the heart. Beneficence vanishes under the criticism of reason, or, at least that of the reason of the Enlightenment; Rousseau uses all his art to make the life of men together attractive not only to the reason but to the affections; he paints for us the nobility, the satisfaction, and the joy of citizenship.

D'Alembert had also suggested in his article that the pastors of Geneva were Socinians, deists and rationalists; this he intended as praise. Rousseau begins his response with a discussion of this problem, and in spite of its apparent irrelevance to the question of the theatre its presence is very much to the point. Although we know that the religion he presents to his Emile goes even further than that of the Socinians in the direction of rationalism, and that Rousseau himself probably went even further than the Savoyard Vicar, he here undertakes the defense of those who still think that belief in the mysteries of revealed religion is legitimate. There is a connection between the position on the theatre of the Encyclopedists and their doctrines concerning religion. Their rationalism presupposed that the maxims of morality could be made clear to all men on the basis of unaided reason. Rousseau appears to deny this. The religious beliefs of a nation are bound up essentially with its practices and its laws; most men are incapable of seeing their real duties without the addition of a religious faith and observance; this faith and observance may very well not be in accordance with what can be proved by universal reason, but it is nonetheless necessary. What can be proved by reason to the majority of men is only the interested calculation of personal benefit and, along with the religion, the citizens' love for one another that Rousseau considered the essence of a real republic would also disappear. The same reasoning which argues that the theatre will civilize men argued in favor of a simply natural religion. The opinion about this higher question, as it were, determines the opinion about the secondary question of the theatre. Rather than having a civilizing effect, he believes that this natural religion would degrade man. Hence he tries to bolster the authority of the pastors who are against the theatre.

The effect of d'Alembert's imputation that the pastors of Geneva were Socinian was to separate them from the pious fundamentalists and to put them willy-nilly in the camp of the more liberal citizens who wanted a theatre. The pastors were thus made to appear heretic to their traditional supporters, besides being intimidated into thinking that the only way to be reasonable and enlightened was to be Socinian. Rousseau protects them against the charge of heresy, but in such a way as not to force them to be strictly orthodox or fundamentalist. He wishes the clergy to be freed from the necessity of making a choice between reason and revelation, a choice forced upon them by the conflict between the traditionalists and the Encyclopedists. He tries to lend the authority of philosophy to a religious teaching based on the belief in revelation; for, if the religious rationalism of the Encyclopedists is accepted, then it is hard to find a defense for the moral commands of the revealed religion which appear to the many to be the only source for obedience to severe laws. Rousseau only touches on this delicate subject in attempting to establish a doctrine which, while incorporating the concern of the Encyclopedists for tolerance as over against fanaticism (a concern which he considered more than legitimate), would not destroy the meaning of the particular religions. He takes a stand for the national religions as over against cosmopolitanism.

Contrary to what might be expected, in establishing his argument against the theatre Rousseau turns neither to the example of primitivism nor to the authority of theology, but to the thought of classical antiquity. More precisely, in opposing the rationalism of the Enlightenment, he does not reject rationalism but supports his position by an older rationalism which did not share the political and moral optimism of the moderns but which still regarded human reason as the only standard. Rousseau draws his arguments chiefly from Plato and points to the possibility of an alternative to the moderns which remains philosophic. Elsewhere this solution may not have appeared adequate to him, but so far as the *Letter to* *d'Alembert* is concerned his argument could have been enunciated by Plato, and we are to understand that, however much he may have differed from the ancients, he believed their articulation of the political phenomena to be far superior to anything since proposed, especially in the crucial area of the arts. The only preparation for the writing of this book which we know Rousseau to have done is that he made a paraphrase of Book X of Plato's *Republic*,* and its influence on the text is evident. The *Letter to d'Alembert* is a comprehensive restatement of a theme which had begun to disappear from the discussion of political theory, a theme which for older thinkers had been central to any study of politics and which revealed the ambiguities of politics better than any other. It is, perhaps, as a clear defense of Plato in terms which reflect the pathos of modernity that this book is most valuable to us; it could well be used as a threshold to enter into classical political theory, which has become so alien to us.

Rousseau divides his treatment of the theatre into three general parts. He begins with a discussion of the effect of dramas on men in general; the issue is whether theatrical beauties play a necessary role in the education of good citizens. Next, he discusses the sort of societies which are required to support a theatre and the general effect of its presence in contrast to that of the institutions it displaces. And, finally, he presents an analysis of the institutions of Geneva and a suggestion about the sorts of entertainments which would most enhance and strengthen its free, republican way of life. He engages in this latter argument in order to provide a model of the true statesmanship of the philosopher, a statesmanship grounded on the consciousness of the inadequacy of universal reasoning to take account of the conditions appropriate to decent political life in particular places.

Rousseau begins with the premise that the theatre is a form of amusement; it exists for the pleasure of those who attend it and, if it hopes in any way to instruct, it must do so by means of the

* *De l'imitation théâtrale*

pleasures. The fact that it is an amusement does not mean that it is a matter of indifference to the legislator; it leads men by what is most immediate and attractive, pleasure, and it is of prime importance to see that the things they take pleasure in are appropriate to a healthy life and that their work and their duties do not conflict with their pleasures. A man must enjoy what he does and love his country in order for him to fulfil his duties and be a citizen who can be relied upon. The best life would be one which provided its own pleasures as a result of its own activity without the need for external sources of amusement; if this is impossible for most men, then those amusements which support and encourage a man in the activities he must perform should be developed. A man whose pleasures bear no relation to the life he leads in the ordinary course of affairs is both miserable and highly untrustworthy; a nation that needs a great number of artificial amusements has lost its taste for its life, and the citizens are likely to be stale and shallow; their activities are not an object of passionate concern and they waste their energies unproductively. The amusements form men's tastes and present them with the objects that appeal most directly to them. The duties of a father, husband, and a citizen are so important and time-consuming that they are bound to suffer when they are no longer a source of pleasure. Because the amusements play such a large role in the formation of character, each one must be examined carefully in its subtle relations to human conduct and to the specific circumstances in which it is to be used before it can be considered admissible. Different countries with different ways of life require different amusements. It is improbable that the universal desirability which d'Alembert attaches to the theatre could be real, for political life implies diversity of national characters; even if the theatre were desirable in itself, the delicate structure of the way of life in any particular country might be undone by importation of alien pleasures. Universal arguments in politics are based on an indifference to the real diversities manifest in it; what men have in common that is politically relevant is not very great and does not include the specific nobility that any one society may embody.

Now, since all amusements appeal to the pleasures of the audiences, their authors are entirely dependent on those audiences for the style and subject matter of their presentation. No matter how excellent the intentions of writers, their works cannot possess a theoretical perfection, for, if nobody comes to see them, if they do not please, they fail entirely. A writer's first rule must be success, and hence he can do nothing that is not wanted by the people. Men cannot be constrained to go to the theatre; the theatre is so revealing precisely because it can only succeed when it touches what is really wanted. Men can be forced to listen to sermons but cannot be forced to enjoy plays. This constitutes the major difference between the thinker and the dramatist; the thinker states the truth as he sees it and is indifferent whether anybody reads him or agrees with him, while the dramatist must appeal to the dominant concerns of the people at large no matter what the status of those concerns might be. Reason has no place in the theatre; drama works through the passions, the very passions which already exist in those who come to it. It may paint some of those passions as ugly, but it cannot paint all of them so; nor will the public permit its dearest desires to be taken lightly, as reason might do; a philosopher on the stage would be absurd or hateful. The drama must awaken the passions; however, it does not necessarily awaken those which have salutary effects, but only those which exist or are dear to the people. A writer can never be in advance of his times; he must be a sensitive instrument reflecting the desires, often still inarticulate, of his age. Even when he presents the most exotic themes he must transform them so that they can move the men of his own time and place; otherwise, such themes will have no meaning for them at all. Although some genius might find a rare and unusual way of moving his audiences and thus manage to avoid some of these difficulties, the theatre is not founded on the rarest talent. A writer who managed to conceal the truth in his works so that only a man of particular wit and intelligence could understand it would be laudable, but his effect on the great mass of mankind would still be the same as that of his fellow authors. The important consideration is that of the rough general effect on the greatest·number of those who are influenced by the theatre, for it is they who create the tone of society. Hence the effect of the theatre is to reinforce national character, to augment the natural inclinations and give a new energy to all of the passions; and from this can be drawn the first general formulation: the theatre is good for good men and bad for bad ones.

Dramatists and critics in former times felt themselves constrained to reflect on the moral effects of the drama in a way which is not always comprehensible to us; they did not believe that whatever an artist does is good or that art has any peculiar value apart from its effect on men. Not only did the intrinsic truth of a work have to be taken into consideration but also whether that truth would be grasped by the public at large; and even if the first conditions were met, there was still the question whether that truth was one which was salutary and a suitable object for special public attention. Rousseau, accordingly, examines the alleged advantages of tragedy and comedy. Tragedy was understood to purge and purify the passions and to provide examples of their dangerous effects. But any man who consults his heart after a tragedy is aware that he is deeply affected and softened. Although great sufferings may be depicted, the high level of intensity and the great joys which accompany them induce men to prefer a life which bears such risks rather than one devoid of both the joys and the sorrows engendered by great passion. And in choosing the passions which he presents as attractive, the author cannot follow his wishes but must accept ours. The habits and tastes of a nation can only be changed in three ways according to Rousseau, by laws, public opinion, and pleasure; and the theatre can make use of none of them to achieve this end: laws are excluded; the theatre must follow public opinion; and the pleasure of theatrical performances can only cause men to come back more often. The tragedy does not teach us to love virtue and to hate vice; for the virtuous and the vicious even to be recognized on the stage, these sentiments must exist beforehand. And all men do prefer virtue to vice in others; that is not the point, but rather, how are we to make them practice virtue? There is no indication that theatregoers perform their duties more punctiliously or readily than non-theatregoers. Furthermore, and this is what is most important, does not the theatre actually remove virtue further from us? Great heroes are surely the models, but what have we to do with heroes? We would be only too glad to share their pleasurable passions, but we do not feel called upon to share their great renunciations, for we do not pretend to be heroes; the passions are made more attractive, while virtue becomes the preserve of special kinds of beings. We learn to cry for others and to applaud our generous souls when we have no sacrifice to make; men are thus given a cheap way to satisfy their moral needs. Men are softened by the tragedy; they hear vice, adorned with the charms of poetry, defended in the mouths of villains; they become accustomed to thinking of the most terrible crimes and to pity those who commit them; they become more indulgent toward their own weakness; and they exhaust their sympathy on alien and distant objects while forgetting their own neighbors and duties. The latter objection could be met by making the drama realistic, but that would destroy its ennobling effect and do away with its instructive purpose. All things considered, the tragedy can, at best, be said to be not a very sure device for improving men.

If tragedy is indifferent, comedy is positively dangerous, for it touches us immediately and with figures much more like those whom we know. It is claimed that comedy makes vice ridiculous and turns men away from it very powerfully for fear of being laughed at. Rousseau denies this effect emphatically; to be ridiculous does not mean to be vicious, for virtue too can be laughed at in many circumstances by the ignorant and the malevolent. The effect of comedy is to attach men more strongly to public opinion, to being sociable rather than virtuous. Duty often requires the courage to be independent of the complacent lethargy of one's fellows, but comedy makes men believe that the worst thing is to be out of step with what is popular; for again, audiences will not laugh at what does not seem funny to them. Virtuous men do not laugh at the vicious; they despise them. Hence, comedy has a tendency to substitute the ridiculous for the vicious and the conventional for the virtuous.

To support this conclusion, Rousseau turns to an analysis of the plays of Molière, an analysis which is one of the most famous and brilliant samples of literary criticism ever written. He accepts the genius of this author and considers him the greatest of all comic poets; he has never voluntarily missed a single performance of any of Molière's works. His very perfection makes him the most favorable case to examine to find out whether the comedy is beneficial to civil society; his intention was the best, but his power is such that if there are harmful effects he will also be able to work them most effectively. The fact is that in all of his plays simplicity is ridiculed and men of the world are favored; the atmosphere of Molière's works is that of sophisticated society where good manners take the place of virtue. One always laughs at pretentious but decent fools, fathers disobeyed, and betrayed husbands. These are the ridiculous people, but the vicious are those who take advantage of them. The net result is that the man influenced by these works would prefer to be thought rather dishonest than an easy dupe; such is the morality of society—shrewdness is preferred to virtue when the two do not coincide.

The best example of Molière's tendency is to be found in his masterpiece, the *Misanthrope*. In this play Molière decided to show in its fullness the ridiculousness of the man who is ridiculous precisely because he is virtuous. Alceste is indeed a virtuous man, for he stands on the best principles and honesty is his only standard; he refuses to make compromises with the manners of his time. He is not a misanthrope in the sense that he does not care for men but because he respects them and regards them as responsible beings, so that he cannot bear their avoidable failings; he is disgusted by those who are obliging to the vicious. This man is opposed to his friend Philinte in the play, who is an easy-going man of the world, taking his bearings by society and unwilling to risk men's displeasure by insisting on standards which most men do not choose to meet. The moral of such a piece can only be to favor an ethic of getting along comfortably, as opposed to the absurd posture of austere insistence on principle. The play is very funny indeed and is all the more blameable for that. But furthermore, Molière actually made some artistic errors in his development of the character. He misrepresented some parts of Alceste's character and did so not because he was unaware of what such a man would really be like but because, if he had been faithful to the misanthrope's nature, his play would have been a great deal less funny. In this way a writer is not only not beneficial to his audience but actually perverts the truth to reach his goal of pleasing. Rousseau identifies himself with the misanthrope, and his act of choosing his civil duties before the proprieties of the Encyclopedists' coterie is laughable from the point of view of men of the world, just as is the misanthrope's intransigent insistence on principle. This is the way the morality of the theatre is opposed to that of citizenship. Molière's successors, without his talent or his probity, ridiculed the most sacred rights and duties and freed men from their awe before them with liberating laughter. So the comedy, too, cannot be said to improve men's morals.

The third head in Rousseau's criticism of the drama is the dominance of the love interest. The ancients rarely used love as a major theme in their tragedies; but with the decadence of the political interest, modern writers have more and more adopted love as the major attraction in their works. But love is the realm of women; it is they who command in it. The result is that all that is considered important must be considered so from the point of view of women's pleasure. This is a reversal of the natural role which women should play in civil society as modest wives and mothers; it gives women the ascendency, tends to corrupt them; and men give up their proper way of life in order to pay their court to women. A man does not think he is really living unless he is in love. The women in the theatre are made to appear wise and virtuous, so that a young man thinks that all he need do is fall in love to become virtuous himself. A society with such a view of women produces denatured ones, as well as men who think of their duty in amorous terms. Furthermore, since old men, who should be the most respectable figures in any sound society, cannot be the lovers and are frequently, because of their position, necessarily opposed to them, they are always represented as fools, villains, or ogres. The effect of such a theatre is to fill Paris with dotards trying to act the parts of swains. What is more, the love interest in plays influences an overpowering passion, one most likely to be in conflict with the responsibilities to country and family. The fact that the loves of the theatre are always decent ones changes nothing; for the awakening of the passion can come from the theatre, but how it will be used depends upon the character of the individual affected by the passion. The proper use of love is perhaps the most important preoccupation of civil society, for it is connected with the family, the source of a state's well- or ill-being, and it is a passion which, if badly trained, can very easily set men at war with their duties. But the playwrights must always make the lover, and the successful lover at that, the most appealing figure in their works; a play which opposed love would meet with ill success. The writer's desire to please sets his interests in opposition to those of the legislator, and the society advocated by the proponents of the theatre would be fit for writers but not for men. There should be no government *by* writers but rather *of* them, for there is not a one-to-one correspondence of their ends with those of civil society. A society without writers might well ask itself if it ought to encourage their presence.

The physical presence of a theatre is bound to change the way of life of a city which did not previously have one; not only does it change the habits of the citizens directly but it requires certain conditions to support it. This fact makes it an object of concern for the legislator even if the effect of the plays were itself beneficial. For the character and the tastes of the people depend upon their habits. The habits of a nation are its all-in-all; they are the cause of the kind of men which it produces, and the production of men who are capable of the best possible life and of being good citizens is the end of statesmanship. The statesman cannot shirk this duty by saying that he will create the conditions of liberty and let each man choose for himself, for a man in an industrial city can hardly lead the life of a pastoral man; moreover, in society our opinions are formed by the dominant opinions of the public, which means that it is highly improbable that a man will have real freedom in his tastes or habits. The true statesman's art is to be able to judge the way of life of his nation and to know which institutions will preserve it and which will destroy it. This is a delicate business and requires a special knowledge of the particular customs of a nation and their relation to its whole way of life. The Encyclopedists have left no role for statesmanship in their universal science. They have sought a political science which would guarantee sound government everywhere, but have forgotten that all that is best in man comes into flower only in very rare circumstances and as a result of extraordinary efforts. These conditions cannot become general; what can become general is only a system of laws and a way of life reflecting a lowered standard of human excellence. The best is not often realized in politics; it is a target to be aimed at, and the means of attaining it vary with the particular people involved. The theatre may be fine, but are the conditions of its existence always compatible with those of a healthy morality? This must be considered, and Rousseau tries to give some latitude to statesmanship that is generally lacking in the thinking of his and our time. The statesman must first judge whether the habits of his country are good or bad and then the sort of effect the theatre will have on them.

Rousseau always takes as his model a small, free republic—Geneva for the moderns, Sparta for the ancients. He wants a city where men can take the most active part in civic life, where the citizens know one another and are most dependent on themselves, where habits of justice, moderation, and courage are required and admired. Can such a city tolerate a theatre? He gives the example of a small community of men living on a mountainside; each owns his own property and lives off its produce; each is sufficient unto himself, for their temperance has kept their needs small; each spends his leisure in making furniture and useful artifices; their entertainments are singing and talking together. A theatre brought among them would produce certain changes: (1) It would turn their attentions and their pleasures away from their work; it would occupy both their time and their thoughts. Not only would it create a certain dissatisfaction with their life as it is, it would also imply that they did less work. (2) They would have to dress well and pay for tickets, which would increase their expenses and make them more dependent on, and in need of, wealth. (3) They would have to build the theatre and make roads to it. These things, not necessary in themselves, would become so as the new pleasures became habits. Hence, taxes would have to be established. (4) And, perhaps most important, the taste for luxury would be introduced. Women who go to the theatre want to appear well and a competition among them always arises. The vanity of women is promoted wherever there are refined entertainments, and their husbands usually support them in it. Adornment becomes an object in itself, and all sorts of expense and attention are devoted to it—not to mention the revolution in family life that is its result. This expense and attention must be given at the sacrifice of other things. In such a community, admittedly a healthy one, the theatre would clearly be pernicious.

Where morals are simple, the people laborious, and their need for relaxation can be satisfied by their own efforts, a theatre should be discouraged by the legislator. But in a big city, full of idle people, where irresponsible and indecent conduct can be hidden by its anonymity, where the people get no satisfaction from their labors, the theatre and all sorts of external pleasures should be encouraged in order to channel the activities of men who would find worse amusements on their own. It is, indeed, possible to construct a civil society where the hard demands of self-imposed restraint are not necessary; a large nation where there is a strong police, an efficient governmental machine, and a populace attached to greedy gain can perhaps function quite efficiently. But such a nation is founded on an indifference to the kind of men who are its citizens; the state is fine, but its matter is contemptible. The theatre in such a nation is not an ennobling force but only an instrument of policy for keeping the subjects amused because they have nothing to do with their liberty and because their training has been such as to prepare them only to abuse it. The theatre is a substitute for virtue; it both helps to avoid certain occasions for the exercise of vice and can practice men in a certain refinement of manners which can make social intercourse easier and more agreeable. Considering the audience to which it is directed, a theatre conceived in this sense is neither a force for the encouragement of virtue nor is it likely to produce great works of art. Rousseau's formulation that the theatre is good in a bad city and bad in a good city means that men admirable in themselves are likely to flourish in cities like Sparta, where literary freedom is clearly contrary to the institutions, while literary freedom is possible only in nations where works of art can only palliate vice and be used for ends wholly dissimilar to those noble ones art sets for itself. The cultivation of minor talents or superficial graces is all that the theatre can promise; this is not undesirable in itself, but talents and graces require moral men to use them if they are not to be pernicious.

The most common objection to the theatre was that actors and actresses are immoral and dissolute and set a bad example. D'Alembert suggested that this danger could be averted by severe laws. But are laws really an answer to such a problem? Laws cannot accomplish everything, and statesmanship consists in finding the laws appropriate to each country; the laws are dependent on the character of a people, not the reverse. Laws instituted in contradiction to public opinion must surely be disobeyed; thus, they not only fail to achieve their end but cause men to have a contempt for law in general. Nor is public opinion fundamentally influenced by reason; it is a result of habit and of countless other factors. Now, the actors will be popular and will be ministers to the pleasures of the people; they will be protected and admired. If this is so, laws cannot control them if they are by nature dissolute; they will gradually transform the law in transforming the people. And Rousseau argues that the contempt that moral men have for actors is no mere prejudice but intimately bound up with their estate. The actor is a man who gives up his own estate to play the roles of others; he has the habit of being all things to all men. This very habit is degrading to a man's dignity, which consists in always being himself. Actors live in a world of illusions and intense passions; such men can rarely be simple, and they hardly fit into a regular way of life. They continually must humiliate themselves pandering to the applause of an anonymous audience. Some of them may be fine men, but the general character of the profession usually molds them. They require a luxurious life and bring it in their wake. The actresses can hardly help being worse, for in addition to having the same disadvantages as the actors, they are women, and attractive ones, and since the specific virtue of women is modesty and actresses must be immodest, they are doubly degraded. They must be immodest because they show themselves off in public, because they live with men, because their whole art is to make themselves attractive and lovable. Modesty is the crown of women, according to Rousseau, and the foundation of the family. There are those rationalists who insist that such modesty is only a social prejudice, but this is only another example of that science which cannot listen to the voice of nature but can only violate it. It is possible to free women and make them like men, but the specific function and charm of women is destroyed, and the men are forced to live lives more like those of women. The actresses, accepted and feted, will have a generally deteriorating effect on morals, and the example of their pleasures will attract many who would have otherwise led virtuous lives. Such are the effects of the theatre: loss of interest in one's own life, luxury, and dissoluteness. Are such habits, Rousseau asks, likely to produce men capable and desirous of sacrificing their pleasures to the hard duties of governing themselves?

And what is the purpose of all this? To create taste. These people will have taste finally, but bad taste. Good taste requires big cities, fine arts, luxury, a highly developed social life, love and debauchery—great vice which must be embellished. It smells of the courts of monarchs. The grace and propriety of a Voltaire will never be found in simple republics. These rustics will only play at being connoisseurs. To have no taste and not to want it is a respectable posture and is not incommensurate with the dignity of a Roman; but to want it and only have bad taste is a ridiculous posture. And, after all, what is this taste so vaunted by the Enlightenment? Knowing all about petty things. This notion of taste was invented to put a veneer on the ugly picture of man painted by Hobbes and accepted by all of Rousseau's contemporaries; it suffices only to trivialize talent and art while corrupting men. Man understood as being motivated by fear of violent death and directed to his comfortable preservation through commerce cannot warm to the exploits of heroism or be attracted by passionate but dangerous loves; the drama will either be a mere diversion for him or he will teach it to tell him stories which encourage his own petty desires. The drama, far from giving man a glory set by the high demands of art and beauty, will be formed by the economics of a philistine and unnatural society. The only way to have true beauty is to have beautiful men and that means free and virtuous men.

In this way Rousseau strikes at the kingpin of the scheme of *l'Encyclopédie*. The freedom from prejudice, and the comfort provided by philosophy and the mechanical arts, respectively, do not present a satisfactory scheme if they are to be used by selfish brutes or esthetes in salons. The taste for the fine arts as understood by the Encyclopedists is not a bright horizon to look to but only a device to make men forget an enslavement of which they are unaware. Only by the uncompromising return to the principles of antiquity, its rationalism and its politics, can man hope for a dignity beyond the self-interested gratification of artificial appetites. Political virtue must come first, and the greatness of the arts, for which Rousseau also pleads, will come later, based on the true greatness of political man.

If reflection on Rousseau's life does not make it clear that he understood the importance of art and science for man, a careful reading of the *Letter to d'Alembert* and the *First Discourse* should suffice to prove it. His work is as much a defense of the arts against a degradation brought on by their popularization as a defense of civil society. The moderns had forgotten nature, and nature teaches that human life has two poles at tension with one another: the life of the mind and the life of the city; this tension is an irreconcilable one, rooted in man's very existence, and it is the very core of Rousseau's thought. Only if one begins by understanding the city as it presents itself naturally, without the admixture of alien doctrines concerning the goodness of the arts, can the problem of the arts emerge in its full clarity. Can there be great art without great men? The misanthrope's morality is that of a sound civil society, one devoted to the training of beautiful citizens; and, if it raises doubts about the goodness of the arts, it is at this point that we must begin to consider their nature. Rousseau's teaching is that the prudence of Lacedaemon cannot be united with the urbanity of Athens, as d'Alembert hoped, unless one wishes to misconstrue them both. This is the source of his sublime self-awareness. Perhaps we moderns have forgotten what the real problem of art is when we smile at the illiberal inconsistency which causes the poet-philosophers Plato and Rousseau to banish poets from their cities.

J.-J. ROUSSEAU

LETTER
TO
M. D'ALEMBERT
ON THE THEATRE

PREFACE

I am at fault if I have on this occasion taken up my pen without necessity. It can be neither advantageous nor agreeable for me to attack M. d'Alembert. I respect his person; I admire his talents; I like his works; I am aware of the good things he has said of my country. Honored myself by his praises, I am in all decency obliged to every sort of consideration for him. But consideration outweighs duty only with those for whom all morality consists in appearances. Justice and truth are man's first duties; humanity and country his first affections. Every time that private considerations cause him to change this order, he is culpable. Could I be culpable in doing what I ought? To answer me one must have a country to serve and more love for his duties than fear of men's displeasure.

Since not everybody has *l'Encyclopédie* before his eyes, I shall here transcribe the passage from the article GENEVA which placed the pen in my hand. The article would have caused the pen to fall from my hand if I aspired to the honor of writing well. But I dare seek another honor in which I fear no one's competition. In reading this passage by itself, more than one reader will be astonished by the zeal which seems to have inspired it; in reading it in the context of the whole article, he will find that the theatre which is not at Geneva, and could be there, takes up one-eighth as much space as do the things which are there.

The drama[2] is not tolerated at Geneva. It is not that they disapprove of the theatre in itself; but they fear, it is said, the taste for adornment, dissipation, and libertinism which the actors' troops disseminate among the youth. However, would it not be possible to remedy this difficulty with laws that are severe and well administered concerning the conduct of the actors? In this way Geneva would have theatre and morals [manners][3], and would enjoy the advantages of both; the theatrical performances would form the taste of the citizens and would give them a fineness of tact, a delicacy of sentiment, which is very difficult to acquire without the help of theatrical performances; literature would profit without the progress of libertinism, and Geneva would join to the prudence of Lacedaemon the urbanity of Athens. Another consideration, worthy of a republic so prudent and so enlightened, ought perhaps to oblige it to permit the theatre. The barbarous prejudice against the actor's profession, the sort of abasement in which we have placed these men so necessary to the progress and support of the arts, is certainly one of the principal causes which contribute to the dissoluteness for which we reproach them. They seek to compensate themselves with pleasure for the esteem which their estate cannot win for them. Among us, an actor with morals [manners] is doubly to be respected, but we hardly take notice of him. The tax-farmer who insults public indigence and feeds himself from it, the courtier who crawls and does not pay his debts, these are the sorts of men we honor the most. If the actors were not only tolerated at Geneva but were first restrained by wise regulations, then protected and even respected when they had earned such respect, and, finally, placed absolutely on the same level as the other citizens, this city would soon have the advantage of possessing what is thought to be so rare and is so only through our fault: a company of actors worthy of esteem. Let us add that this company would soon become Europe's best; many persons, full of taste and capacity for the theatre and who fear being dishonored among us if they devoted themselves to it, would flock to Geneva to cultivate, not only without shame but even with esteem, a talent so agreeable and so infrequent. This city, which many Frenchmen consider dull because they are deprived of the theatre, would then become the seat of decent pleasures, just as it is now the seat of philosophy and liberty; and foreigners would no longer be surprised to see that in a city where proper and correct theatre is forbidden, coarse and silly farces as contrary to good taste as to good morals [manners] are permitted. This is not all: little by little the example of Geneva's actors, the correctness of their conduct and the respect which it would cause them to enjoy, would serve as a model to the actors of other nations and as a lesson to those who have treated them until now with so much severity and even inconsistency. One would no longer see them, on the one hand, being pensioned by the government and, on the other, as objects of anathema; our priests would lose the habit of excommunicating them, and our men of the middle class of regarding them with contempt; and a little republic would have the glory of having reformed Europe on this point, which is perhaps more important than is thought.

This is certainly the most agreeable and seductive picture that could be offered us, but is, at the same time, the most dangerous advice that could be given us. At least, such is my sentiment, and my reasons are in this writing. With what avidity will the young of Geneva, swept away by so weighty an authority, give themselves to ideas for which they already have only too great a penchant? Since the publication of this volume, how many young Genevans, otherwise good citizens, are waiting for the moment to promote the establishment of a theatre, believing that they are rendering a service to their country and, almost, to humankind? This is the subject of my alarm; this is the ill that I would fend off. I do justice to the intentions of M. d'Alembert; I hope he will do the same in regard to mine. I have no more desire to displease him than he to do us injury. But, finally, even if mistaken, must I not act and speak according to my conscience and my lights? Ought I to have remained silent? Could I have, without betraying my duty and my country?

To have the right to remain silent on this occasion, I should need never to have raised my pen for subjects less necessary. Sweet obscurity, which was for thirty years my happiness, I should need always to have known how to love thee. It would have to be unknown that I have had some relations with the editors of *l'Encyclopédie*, that I have furnished some articles for the work, that my name is to be found with those of the authors. My zeal for my country would have to be less known, and it would be necessary that others supposed that the article *Geneva* had escaped my attention or that they could not infer from my silence that I adhere to its contents. Since none of this is possible, I must then speak; I must disavow what I cannot at all approve, so that sentiments other than my own cannot be imputed to me. My countrymen have no need of my advice; I know it well. But I have need to do myself honor in showing that I think as they do about our maxims.

I am not unaware that this writing, so far from what it ought to be, is far even from what I could have done in happier days. So many things have concurred to put it beneath the mediocrity to which I could in the past attain that I am surprised that it is not even worse. I wrote for my country; if it were true that zeal takes the place of talent, I would have done better than ever; but I have seen what needed to be done, and could not bring it to execution. I have spoken the truth coldly; who cares for the truth? Dreary recommendation for a book! To be useful, one must be charming, and my pen has lost that art. Some will malignantly contest this loss. Be that as it may; nevertheless, I feel that I am fallen, and one cannot sink beneath nothingness.

In the first place, I am not dealing here with vain philosophical chatter but with a practical truth important to a whole people. I do not speak here to the few but to the public, nor do I attempt to make others think but rather to explain my thought clearly. Hence, I had to change my style. To make myself better understood by everyone, I have said fewer things with more words; and wanting to be clear and simple, I have found myself loose and diffuse.

At first I counted on one or two printed pages at the very most. I began in a hurry and, my subject expanding itself under my pen, I let it go without constraint. I was sick and melancholy, and although I had great need of distraction, I felt myself so little in a state to think or write that, if the idea of a duty to fulfil had not sustained me, I would have thrown my paper in the fire a hundred times. As a result I became less severe with myself. I sought some enjoyment in my work that I might bear it. I plunged myself into every digression which presented itself, without foreseeing to what extent I, in relieving my boredom, was perhaps providing for that of the reader.

Taste, selectiveness, and correctness are not to be found in this work. Living alone, I have not been able to show it to anyone. I had an Aristarchus,[4] severe and judicious. I have him no more; I want him no more;* but I will regret him unceasingly, and my heart misses him even more than my writings.

Solitude calms the soul and appeases the passions born of the disorder of the world. Far from the vices which irritate us, we speak of them with less indignation; far from the ills which touch us, our hearts are less moved by them. Since I see men no more, I have almost stopped hating the wicked. Moreover, the ill they have done me deprives me of the right to speak ill of them. Henceforth, I must pardon them so as not to resemble them. I would substitute unawares the love of justice for the love of vengeance. It is better to forget all. I hope that that bitterness will no longer be found for which I was reproached but which caused me to be read; I agree to be less read, provided that I live in peace.

To these reasons is added another and yet crueler one that I would in vain like to hide; the public would sense it only too well in spite of me. If among the essays issued from my pen this paper is even beneath the others, it is less the fault of circumstances than of myself; I am beneath myself. The ills of the body exhaust the soul; by dint of suffering it loses its vitality. A fleeting moment of fermentation produced a certain glimmer of talent in me. It manifested itself late, and it has extinguished itself early. In returning to my natural state, I have gone back to nothingness. I had only a moment; it is past. It is my shame to outlive myself. Reader, if you receive this last work with indulgence, you will be welcoming my shade, for, as for me, I am no more.

Montmorenci, March 20, 1758

* *Ad amicum etsi produxeris gladium, non desperes; est enim regressus ad amicum. Si aperueris os triste, non timeas: est enim concordatio: excepto convitio; et improperio, et superbia, et mysterii revelatione, et plaga dolosa. In his omnibus effugiet amicus* (Ecclesiasticus XXII, 26–27).[5]

J.-J. ROUSSEAU
CITIZEN OF GENEVA
TO
MONSIEUR D'ALEMBERT

I

I have read, Sir, with pleasure your article, *Geneva*, in the 7th volume of *l'Encyclopédie*. In rereading it with even more pleasure, it has provided me with some reflections which I thought I could offer, under your auspices, to the public and my fellow citizens. There is much to commend in this article; but, if the praises with which you have honored my country deprive me of the right to make return in kind, my sincerity will speak for me; not to be of your opinion on some points is to make myself clear enough about the others.

I shall begin with what is for me most repugnant to treat and the consideration of which is least appropriate for me, but about which, for the reason I have just mentioned, silence is not permitted me. This is the judgment that you make about the doctrine of our ministers in the matter of faith.[6] You have praised this worthy body in a way that is very fair, very true, and appropriate to it alone among all the clergies of the world, in a way which yet increases the respect for you of which they have given witness; you have praised them, showing that they love philosophy and do not fear the eye of the philosopher. But, Sir, when one wishes to honor people, it must be done after their fashion and not our own, lest, with reason, they be offended by harmful praises which, for all that they are given with good intention, nonetheless do damage to the estate, the interests, the opinions, or the prejudices of those who are their object. Are you unaware that every sectarian name is always odious and that such imputations, rarely without consequence for the laity, are never so for theologians?

You will tell me that it is a question of facts and not praises and that the philosopher has more respect for the truth than for men. But this pretended truth is not so clear or so indifferent that you have the right to advance it without good authorities; and I do not see on what one could found oneself to prove that the sentiments that a group professes and according to which it acts are not its own. You will tell me next that you do not attribute the sentiments of which you speak to the whole ecclesiastical body. But you do attribute them to many; and many, in a small number, always compose such a large part that the whole must be affected by them.

Many pastors of Geneva have, according to you, only a complete Socinianism.[7] This is what you declare boldly to the face of Europe. I dare to ask you how you learned it? It can only be from your own conjectures or from the witness of others or from the confession of the pastors in question.

Now, in matters of pure dogma, which have nothing at all to do with morality, how can one judge another's faith by conjecture? How can one even judge it on the assertion of a third party against that of the interested party? Who knows better than I what I do or do not believe? And to whom ought one to refer on this point other than myself? When, after having drawn sophistical and disclaimed consequences from the speeches or writings of a decent man, a fierce priest persecutes the author for these consequences, he is only performing his priest's profession and surprises no one. But ought we to honor virtuous men the way a knave persecutes them? And will the philosopher imitate the captious reasonings of which he was so often the victim?

There remains then the possibility that those of our pastors whom you allege to be complete Socinians and to reject eternal punishments have confided their private sentiments on this score to you. But if this were really their sentiment and they had confided it to you, they certainly would have told you in secret, in the decent and frank expansiveness of philosophic intercourse; they would have said it to the philosopher and not to the author. They did nothing of the sort, and my proof is without reply: it is that you published it.

I do not claim, for that, either to judge or to blame the doctrine that you impute to them; I say only that one has no right to impute it to them, at least unless they admit it; and, I add, that it does not resemble the one in which they instruct us at all. I do not know what Socinianism is, so that I can speak neither well nor ill of it (and, indeed, from a few confused notions of this sect and its founder, I feel more disinclination than taste for it).[8] But, in general, I am the friend of every peaceful religion in which the Eternal Being is served according to the reason he gave us. When a man cannot believe what he finds absurd, it is not his fault; it is that of his reason.* And how shall I conceive that God would punish him

---

* I think I see a principle, which, well demonstrated as it could be, would immediately wrest the arms from the hands of the intolerant and the superstitious and would calm that proselytizing fury which seems to animate the unbelievers. This is that human reason has no well-determined common measure and that it is unjust for any man to give his own as the rule to that of others.

Let us suppose good faith, without which all disputation is only cackle. Up to a certain point there are common principles, a common evidence, and, in addition, each has his own reason which determines him; thus this sentiment does not lead to scepticism; but also, since the general limits of reason are not fixed and no one can inspect another's, here, with one stroke, the proud dogmatist is stopped. If ever peace could be established where interest, pride, and opinionation now reign, thereby the dissensions of the priests and the philosophers would finally end. But perhaps it would be to the advantage of neither the one nor the other; there would be neither persecutions nor disputations any more; the former would have no one to torment, the latter no one to convince: one might as well leave the trade.

If I should be asked why then I myself dispute, I would answer that I speak to the many and that I am explaining practical truths, that I base myself on experience, that I am fulfilling my duty, and that, after having said what I think, I see no harm in it if my opinion is not accepted.

for not having made for himself an understanding* contrary to the one he received from Him? If a learned man came and ordered me on behalf of God to believe that the part is greater than the whole, what could I think within myself other than that this man came to order me to be mad? Certainly the orthodox, who see no absurdity in the mysteries, are obliged to believe them. But if the Socinians find the mysteries absurd, what can be said to them? Will it be proved to them that they are not? They will begin by proving to you that it is an absurdity to reason about what cannot be understood. What to do, then? Leave them alone.

Nor am I scandalized that those who serve a merciful God reject eternal punishment if they find it incompatible with his justice. If in such cases they interpret as best they can the passages contrary to their opinion rather than abandon it, how could they do otherwise? No one is more filled than I with love and respect for the

---

* It must be remembered that I am answering an author who is not Protestant; and I believe I really answer him in showing that what he accuses our ministers of doing would be done to no avail in our religion and is necessarily done in many others unawares.

The intellectual world, without excepting geometry, is full of truths incomprehensible and nevertheless incontestable; because reason, which demonstrates their existence, cannot, as it were, touch them across the limits which arrest it but can only perceive them at a distance. Such is the dogma of the existence of God; such are the mysteries admitted in the Protestant communions. The mysteries which shock reason, to employ the terms of M. d'Alembert, are an entirely different matter. Their very contradiction makes them return within the limits of reason; it has every imaginable advantage for making felt that they do not exist; for, although one cannot see an absurd thing, nothing is so clear as absurdity. This is what happens when two contradictory propositions are maintained: if you tell me that a space of one inch is also a space of one foot, you do not say something that is mysterious, obscure, and incomprehensible; you assert, on the contrary, a glaring and palpable absurdity, a thing *very clearly* false. Of whatever sort the demonstrations which establish it are, they are unable to outweigh the one which undermines it, for this principle is drawn immediately from the primitive notions which serve as the basis of every human certitude. Otherwise, reason giving witness against itself would force us to renounce it. And far from making us believe this or that, it would prevent us from believing anything at all, considering that every principle of faith would be destroyed. Any man, of whatever religion he be, who claims to believe in such mysteries is either an impostor or does not know what he says.

most sublime of all books; it consoles me and instructs me every day, when other books inspire in me only disgust. But I maintain that, if the Scripture itself gave us some idea of God unworthy of Him, we would have to reject it on that point, just as you reject in geometry the demonstrations which lead to absurd conclusions. For, of whatever authenticity the sacred text may be, it is still more believable that the Bible was altered than that God is unjust or malevolent.

These, Sir, are the reasons which would prevent me from blaming these sentiments in equitable and moderate theologians who, by their own doctrine, would teach that no one should be forced to adopt it. I will say more; ways of thinking so appropriate for a reasonable and feeble creature, so worthy of a just and merciful creator, appear to me preferable to that stupid acceptance which makes an animal out of man, and to that barbarous intolerance which delights in tormenting, already in this life, those whom it destines to eternal torments in the next. In this sense, I thank you, on behalf of my country, for the spirit of philosophy and humanity that you recognize in its clergy and for the justice you are pleased to do it. I am in agreement with you on this point. But for being humane, philosophic, and tolerant,* it does not follow that the members of the clergy are heretic. In the party name you give them, in the dogmas that you say are theirs, I can neither agree with you nor follow you. Although such a system may perhaps have nothing that does not do honor to those who adopt it, I will refrain from attributing it to my pastors who have not adopted it, for fear that the praise I might make of it would provide others with the subject for a very grave accusation and would hurt those I had pretended to praise. Why should I take the responsibility for

* Concerning Christian tolerance, the chapter which bears this title can be consulted in the eleventh book of Professor Vernet's *Doctrine chrétienne*.[9] There it can be seen for what reasons the Church ought to use even more caution and circumspection in the censure of errors concerning the faith than in that of errors concerning morals [manners], and how the gentleness of the Christian, the reason of the wise man, and the zeal of the pastor are combined in the rules of this censorship.

another's profession of faith? Have I not learned only too well to fear these rash imputations! How many people have taken the responsibility for my faith in accusing me of lacking in religion, people who have surely read my heart very badly? I shall not tax them with lacking religion themselves. For one of the duties it imposes on me is to respect the secrets of consciences. Sir, let us judge the actions of men and leave it to God to judge of their faith.

This is perhaps too much on a point whose examination does not belong to me and which, moreover, is not the subject of this letter. The ministers of Geneva have no need of another's pen to defend themselves.* It is not mine that they would choose for that, and such discussions are too far from my inclination for me to give myself to them with pleasure. But, since I have to speak about the same article in which you attribute opinions to them which we do not know to be theirs, to remain silent about this assertion was to appear to adhere to it; and that I am very far from doing. Aware of the good fortune that we have in possessing a body of philosophic and pacific theologians, or rather a body of officers of morality** and ministers of virtue, I view with consternation any occasion which might cause them to descend to being mere churchmen. It is of import for us to preserve them such as they are. It is of import for us that they themselves enjoy the peace which they

* This is what they have just done, according to what I have been written, in a public declaration.[10] It has not yet come to me in my retreat; but I learn that the public has received it with applause. Thus not only do I have the pleasure of having been the first to do them the honor they deserve but also that of hearing my judgment unanimously confirmed. I realize that this declaration renders the beginning of my letter entirely superfluous and in any other case would perhaps make it indiscreet. But, on the point of suppressing it, I saw that, speaking of the same article which gave occasion to the letter, the same reason still existed and that my silence could be taken for a sort of agreement. I leave, then, these reflections, so much the more willingly; for, if they are presented out of context concerning an affair that is happily ended, they contain nothing in general that is not honorable to the church of Geneva and useful to men in all lands.

** It is thus that the Abbé de St. Pierre always called the ecclesiastics, either to say that this is what they really are or to make clear that this is what they ought to be.

make us love, and that odious disputes of theology trouble no more either their repose or ours. It is of import for us, finally, always to learn from their lessons and their example that gentleness and humanity are also the virtues of the Christian.

II

I HASTEN to turn to a discussion that is less grave and less serious but which is still of enough concern to us to merit our reflection and which I enter into more willingly as it is somewhat more within my competence. It is that of the project to establish a theatre for the drama at Geneva. I shall not expound here my conjectures about the motives which might have brought you to propose an establishment so contrary to our maxims. Whatever your reasons, I have here to do only with ours; and all that I shall permit myself to say with respect to you is that you will surely be the first philosopher* who ever encouraged a free people, a small city, and a poor state to burden itself with a public theatre.[12]

How many questions I find to discuss in what you appear to have settled! Whether the theatre is good or bad in itself? Whether it can be united with morals [manners]? Whether it is in conformity with republican austerity? Whether it ought to be tolerated in a little city? Whether the actor's profession can be a decent one? Whether actresses can be as well behaved as other women? Whether good laws suffice for repressing the abuses? Whether these laws can be well observed? etc. Everything is still problematic concerning the real effects of the theatre; for, since the disputes that it occasions are solely between the men of the church and the men of the world, each side views the problem only through its

* Of two famous historians, both philosophers, both dear to M. d'Alembert, the modern[11] would be of his opinion, perhaps; but Tacitus, whom he loves, about whom he meditates, whom he deigns to translate, the grave Tacitus, whom he quotes so willingly, and whom he sometimes imitates so well except for his obscurity, would he have agreed?

prejudices. Here, Sir, are studies that would not be unworthy of your pen. As for me, without believing that what I might do could serve as a substitute for your efforts, I shall limit myself in this essay to seeking those clarifications that you have made necessary. I beg you to take into consideration that in speaking my opinion in imitation of your example, I am fulfilling a duty toward my country, and that, if my sentiments are mistaken, at least this error can hurt no one.

At the first glance given to these institutions I see immediately that the theatre is a form of amusement; and if it is true that amusements are necessary to man, you will at least admit that they are only permissible insofar as they are necessary, and that every useless amusement is an evil for a being whose life is so short and whose time is so precious. The state of man has its pleasures which are derived from his nature and are born of his labors, his relations, and his needs. And these pleasures, sweeter to the one who tastes them in the measure that his soul is healthier, make whoever is capable of participating in them indifferent to all others. A father, a son, a husband, and a citizen have such cherished duties to fulfil that they are left nothing to give to boredom. The good use of time makes time even more precious, and the better one puts it to use, the less one can find to lose. Thus it is constantly seen that the habit of work renders inactivity intolerable and that a good conscience extinguishes the taste for frivolous pleasures. But it is discontent with one's self, the burden of idleness, the neglect of simple and natural tastes, that makes foreign amusement so necessary. I do not like the need to occupy the heart constantly with the stage as if it were ill at ease inside of us. Nature itself dictated the response of that barbarian* to whom were vaunted the magnificences of the circus and the games established at Rome. "Don't the Romans," asked this fellow, "have wives or children?" The barbarian was right. People think they come together in the theatre,

* Chrysost. in Matth. Homel, 38.

and it is there that they are isolated. It is there that they go to forget their friends, neighbors, and relations in order to concern themselves with fables, in order to cry for the misfortunes of the dead, or to laugh at the expense of the living. But I should have sensed that this language is no longer seasonable in our times. Let us try to find another which is better understood.

To ask if the theatre is good or bad in itself is to pose too vague a question; it is to examine a relation before having defined the terms. The theatre is made for the people, and it is only by its effects on the people that one can determine its absolute qualities. There can be all sorts of entertainment.* There is, from people to people, a prodigious diversity of morals [manners], tempera-ments, and characters. Man is one; I admit it! But man modified by religions, governments, laws, customs, prejudices, and climates be-comes so different from himself that one ought not to seek among us for what is good for men in general, but only what is good for them in this time or that country. Thus the plays of Menander, made for the Athenian theatre, were out of place in Rome's. Thus the gladiatorial combats which, during the republic, animated the courage and valor of the Romans, only inspired the population of Rome, under the emperors, with the love of blood and cruelty. The same object offered to the same people at different times taught

* "There can be entertainments blameable in themselves, like those which are inhuman or indecent and licentious; such were some of the pagan enter-tainments. But there are also some which are indifferent in themselves and only become bad through their abuse. For example, theatrical plays are not objectionable insofar as in them descriptions are to be found of the characters and actions of men, where agreeable and useful lessons for every station in life can even be presented. But if an easygoing morality is retailed in them; if the people who exercise this profession lead a licentious life and serve to corrupt others; if such shows support vanity, idleness, luxury, and lewdness, it is evi-dent that the thing turns into an abuse; and unless a way is found to correct these abuses or to protect ourselves from them, it is better to give up this form of amusement." (*Instruction chrétienne*,[13] Vol. III, Book iii, ch. 16.)

This is the state of the question when it is well posed. What must be known is whether the morality of the theatre is necessarily easygoing, whether the abuses are inevitable, whether its difficulties are derived from the nature of the thing or whether they come from causes that can be set aside.

men at first to despise their own lives and, later, to make sport of the lives of others.

The sorts of entertainment are determined necessarily by the pleasure they give and not by their utility. If utility is there too, so much the better. But the principal object is to please; and, provided that the people enjoy themselves, this object is sufficiently attained. This alone will always prevent our being able to give these sorts of institutions all the advantages they are susceptible of; and it is a gross self-deception to form an idea of perfection for them that could not be put into practice without putting off those whom one wants to instruct. It is from this that is born the diversity of entertainments according to the diverse tastes of nations. An intrepid, grave, and cruel people wants deadly and perilous festivals in which valor and composure shine. A ferocious and intense people wants blood, combat, and terrible passions. A voluptuous people wants music and dances. A gallant[14] people wants love and civility. A frivolous people wants joking and ridicule. *Trahit sua quemque voluptas.*[15] To please them, there must be entertainments which promote their penchants, whereas what is needed are entertainments which would moderate them.

The stage is, in general, a painting of the human passions, the original of which is in every heart. But if the painter neglected to flatter these passions, the spectators would soon be repelled and would not want to see themselves in a light which made them despise themselves. So that, if he gives an odious coloring to some passions, it is only to those that are not general and are naturally hated. Hence the author, in this respect, only follows public sentiment. And then, these repulsive passions are always used to set off others, if not more legitimate, at least more to the liking of the spectators. It is only reason that is good for nothing on the stage. A man without passions or who always mastered them could not attract anyone. And it has already been observed that a Stoic in tragedy would be an insufferable figure. In comedy he would, at most, cause laughter.

Let no one then attribute to the theatre the power to change sentiments or morals [manners], which it can only follow and embellish. An author who would brave the general taste would soon write for himself alone. When Molière transformed the comic stage, he attacked modes and ridiculous traits. But, for all of that, he did not shock the public's taste.* He followed or expanded on it, just as Corneille, on his part, did. It was the old theatre which was beginning to shock this taste, because, in an age grown more refined, the theatre preserved its initial coarseness. So, also, the general taste having changed since the time of these two authors, if their masterpieces were now to be presented for the first time, they would inevitably fail. The connoisseurs can very well admire them forever; if the public still admires them, it is more for shame at recanting than from a real sentiment for their beauties. It is said that a good play never fails. Indeed, I believe it; this is because a good play never shocks the morals [manners]** of its time. Who doubts that the best play of Sophocles would fall flat in our theatre? We would be unable to put ourselves in the places of men who are totally dissimilar to us.

Any author who wants to depict alien morals [manners] for us nevertheless takes great pains to make his play correspond to our morals [manners]. Without this precaution, one never succeeds,

* Although he anticipated public taste by only a bit, Molière himself had difficulty in succeeding; the most perfect of his works failed at its birth because he presented it too soon and the public was not yet ripe for the *Misanthrope*.

All of this is founded on an evident maxim, i.e., that a people often follows practices which it despises or which it is ready to despise as soon as someone dares to set the example for it. When, in my day, the puppet rage was ridiculed, what was said in the theatre was only the reflection of what was thought by even those who spent their days at that silly amusement. But the constant tastes of a people, its customs, its old prejudices, ought to be respected on the stage. Never has a poet come off well who violated this law.

** I say the tastes or morals [manners] indifferently. For although the one is not the other, they always have a common origin and undergo the same revolutions. This does not imply that good taste and good morals [manners] always reign at the same time; this is an assertion which requires clarification and discussion. But that a certain state of taste always answers to a certain state of morals [manners] is indisputable.

and even the success of those who have taken it often has grounds very different from those supposed by a superficial observer. If the *Arlequin sauvage*[16] is so well received by audiences, is it thought that this is a result of their taste for the character's sense and simplicity, or that a single one of them would want to resemble him? It is, all to the contrary, that this play appeals to their turn of mind, which is to love and seek out new and singular ideas. Now there is nothing newer for them than what has to do with nature. It is precisely their aversion for the ordinary which sometimes leads them back to the simple things.

It follows from these first observations that the general effect of the theatre is to strengthen the national character, to augment the natural inclinations, and to give a new energy to all the passions. In this sense it would seem that, its effect being limited to intensifying and not changing the established morals [manners], the drama would be good for the good and bad for the vicious. Even in the first case it would remain to be seen if the passions did not degenerate into vices from being too much excited. I know that the poetic theatre claims to do exactly the opposite and to purge the passions in exciting them. But I have difficulty understanding this rule. Is it possible that in order to become temperate and prudent we must begin by being intemperate and mad?

"Oh no! It is not that," say the partisans of the theatre. "Tragedy certainly intends that all the passions which it portrays move us; but it does not always want our emotion to be the same as that of the character tormented by a passion. More often, on the contrary, its purpose is to excite sentiments in us opposed to those it lends its characters." They say, moreover, that if authors abuse their power of moving hearts to excite an inappropriate interest, this fault ought to be attributed to the ignorance and depravity of the artists and not to the art. They say, finally, that the faithful depiction of the passions and of the sufferings which accompany them suffices in itself to make us avoid them with all the care of which we are capable.

To become aware of the bad faith of all these responses, one need only consult his own heart at the end of a tragedy. Do the emotion, the disturbance, and the softening which are felt within onself and which continue after the play give indication of an immediate disposition to master and regulate our passions? Are the lively and touching impressions to which we become accustomed and which return so often, quite the means to moderate our sentiments in the case of need? Why should the image of the sufferings born of the passions efface that of the transports of pleasure and joy which are also seen to be born of them and which the authors are careful to adorn even more in order to render their plays more enjoyable? Do we not know that all the passions are sisters and that one alone suffices for arousing a thousand, and that to combat one by the other is only the way to make the heart more sensitive to them all? The only instrument which serves to purge them is reason, and I have already said that reason has no effect in the theatre. It is true that we do not share the feelings of all the characters; for, since their interests are opposed, the author must indeed make us prefer one of them; otherwise we would have no contact at all with the play. But far from choosing, for that reason, the passions which he wants to make us like, he is forced to choose those which we like already. What I have said of the sorts of entertainment ought to be understood even more of the interest which is made dominant in them. At London a drama is interesting when it causes the French to be hated; at Tunis, the noble passion would be piracy; at Messina, a delicious revenge; at Goa, the honor of burning Jews. If an author* shocks these maxims, he will write a very fine play to which no one will go. And then this author must be taxed with

* In order to see this, let a man, righteous and virtuous, but simple and crude, with neither love nor gallantry and who speaks no fine phrases, be put on the French stage; let a prudent man without prejudices be put on it, one who, having been affronted by a bully, refuses to go and have his throat cut by the offender; and let the whole theatrical art be exhausted in rendering these characters as appealing to the French people as is the Cid: I will be wrong, if it succeeds.

ignorance, with having failed in the first law of his art, in the one
which serves as the basis for all the others, which is, to succeed.
Thus the theatre purges the passions that one does not have and
foments those that one does. Is that a well-administered remedy?

Hence, there is a combination of general and particular causes
which keeps the theatre from being given that perfection of which
it is thought to be susceptible and from producing the advantageous
effects that seem to be expected from it. Even if this perfection is
supposed to be as great as it can be, and the people as well disposed
as could be wished, nevertheless these effects would be reduced to
nothing for want of means to make them felt. I know of only three
instruments with which the morals [manners] of a people can be
acted upon: the force of the laws, the empire of opinion, and the
appeal of pleasure. Now the laws have no access to the theatre
where the least constraint would make it a pain and not an amusement.* Opinion does not depend on the theatre, since, rather than
giving the law to the public, the theatre receives the law from it.
And, as to the pleasure that can be had in the theatre, its whole
effect is to bring us back more often.

Let us see if there can be other means. The theatre, I am told,
directed as it can and ought to be, makes virtue lovable and vice
odious. What? Before there were dramas, were not virtuous men
loved, were not the vicious hated, and are these sentiments feebler
in the places that lack a theatre? The theatre makes virtue lovable
. . . It accomplishes a great miracle in doing what nature and
reason do before it! The vicious are hated on the stage . . . . . Are
they loved in society when they are known to be such? Is it quite
certain that this hate is the work of the author rather than of the
crimes that he makes the vicious commit? Is it quite certain that

* The laws can determine the subjects of the plays, and their form, and
the way to play them; but the laws cannot force the public to enjoy them.
The emperor Nero sang at the theatre and had all those who fell asleep put
to death; still he could not keep everybody awake. And the pleasure of a
short nap came close to costing Vespasian his life.[17] Noble Actors of the
Paris Opera, if you had enjoyed the imperial power, I should not now complain about having lived too long.

the simple account of these crimes would produce less horror in us than all the colors with which he has painted them? If his whole art consists in producing malefactors for us in order to render them hateful, I am unable to see what is so admirable in this art, and we get, in this regard, only too many lessons without need of this one. Dare I add a suspicion which comes to me? I suspect that any man, to whom the crimes of Phaedra or Medea were told beforehand, would hate them more at the beginning of the play than at the end. And if this suspicion is well founded, then what are we to think of this much-vaunted effect of the theatre?

I should like to be clearly shown, without wasting words, how it could produce sentiments in us that we did not have and could cause us to judge moral beings otherwise than we judge them by ourselves? How puerile and senseless are these vain pretensions when examined closely! If the beauty of virtue were the product of art, virtue would have long since been disfigured! As for me, even if I am again to be regarded as wicked for daring to assert that man is born good, I think it and believe that I have proved it. The source of the concern which attaches us to what is decent and which inspires us with aversion for evil is in us and not in the plays. There is no art for producing this concern, but only for taking advantage of it. The love of the beautiful* is a sentiment as natural to the human heart as the love of self; it is not born out of an arrangement of scenes; the author does not bring it; he finds it there; and out of this pure sentiment, to which he appeals, are born the sweet tears that he causes to flow.

Imagine a play as perfect as you like. Where is the man who, going for the first time, does not go already convinced of what is to be proved in it and already predisposed toward those whom he is

---

* We have to do with the morally beautiful here. Whatever the philosophers may say of it, this love is innate to man and serves as principle to his conscience. (I can cite as an example of this the little play *Nanine,* which has caused the audience to grumble and is only protected by the great reputation of its author.[18] All this is only because honor, virtue, and the pure sentiments of nature are preferred in it to the impertinent prejudice of social station.)

meant to like? But this is not the question; what is important is to act consistently with one's principles and to imitate the people whom one esteems. The heart of man is always right concerning that which has no personal relation to himself. In the quarrels at which we are purely spectators, we immediately take the side of justice, and there is no act of viciousness which does not give us a lively sentiment of indignation so long as we receive no profit from it. But when our interest is involved, our sentiments are soon corrupted. And it is only then that we prefer the evil which is useful to us to the good that nature makes us love. Is it not a necessary effect of the constitution of things that the vicious man profits doubly, from his injustice and the probity of others? What more advantageous treaty could he conclude than one obliging the whole world, excepting himself, to be just, so that everyone will faithfully render unto him what is due him, while he renders to no one what he owes? He loves virtue, unquestionably; but he loves it in others because he hopes to profit from it. He wants none of it for himself because it would be costly to him. What then does he go to see at the theatre? Precisely what he wants to find everywhere: lessons of virtue for the public, from which he excepts himself, and people sacrificing everything to their duty while nothing is exacted from him.

I hear it said that tragedy leads to pity through fear. So it does; but what is this pity? A fleeting and vain emotion which lasts no longer than the illusion which produced it; a vestige of natural sentiment soon stifled by the passions; a sterile pity which feeds on a few tears and which has never produced the slightest act of humanity. Thus, the sanguinary Sulla cried at the account of evils he had not himself committed.[19] Thus, the tyrant of Phera hid himself at the theatre for fear of being seen groaning with Andromache and Priam, while he heard without emotion the cries of so many unfortunate victims slain daily by his orders.[20] Tacitus reports that Valerius Asiaticus, calumniously accused by the order of Messalina, who wanted him to perish, defended himself before the emperor in a way that touched this prince very deeply and drew tears from Messalina herself. She went into the next room in order to regain her composure after having, in the midst of her tears, whispered a warning to Vitellius not to let the accused escape. I never see one of these weeping ladies in the boxes at the theatre, so proud of their tears, without thinking of the tears of Messalina for the poor Valerius Asiaticus.[21]

If, according to the observation of Diogenes Laertius, the heart is more readily touched by feigned ills than real ones, if theatrical imitations draw forth more tears than would the presence of the objects imitated, it is less because the emotions are feebler and do not reach the level of pain, as the Abbé du Bos believes,* than because they are pure and without mixture of anxiety for ourselves. In giving our tears to these fictions, we have satisfied all the rights of humanity without having to give anything more of ourselves; whereas unfortunate people in person would require attention from us, relief, consolation, and work, which would involve us in their pains and would require at least the sacrifice of our indolence, from all of which we are quite content to be exempt. It could be said that our heart closes itself for fear of being touched at our expense.

In the final accounting, when a man has gone to admire fine actions in stories and to cry for imaginary miseries, what more can be asked of him? Is he not satisfied with himself? Does he not applaud his fine soul? Has he not acquitted himself of all that he owes to virtue by the homage which he has just rendered it? What more could one want of him? That he practice it himself? He has no role to play; he is no actor.

The more I think about it, the more I find that everything that is played in the theatre is not brought nearer to us but made more

* He says that the poet afflicts us only so much as we wish, that he makes us like his heroes only so far as it pleases us.[22] This is contrary to all experience. Many people refrain from going to tragedy because they are moved to the point of discomfort; others, ashamed of crying at the theatre, do so nevertheless in spite of themselves; and these effects are not rare enough to be only exceptions to the maxim of this author.

distant. When I see the *Comte d'Essex*,[23] the reign of Elizabeth is ten centuries removed in my eyes, and, if an event that took place yesterday at Paris were played, I should be made to suppose it in the time of Molière. The theatre has rules, principles, and a morality apart, just as it has a language and a style of dress that is its own. We say to ourselves that none of this is suitable for us, and that we should think ourselves as ridiculous to adopt the virtues of its heroes as it would be to speak in verse or to put on Roman clothing. This is pretty nearly the use of all these great sentiments and of all these brilliant maxims that are vaunted with so much emphasis—to relegate them forever to the stage, and to present virtue to us as a theatrical game, good for amusing the public but which it would be folly seriously to attempt introducing into society. Thus the most advantageous impression of the best tragedies is to reduce all the duties of man to some passing and sterile emotions that have no consequences, to make us applaud our courage in praising that of others, our humanity in pitying the ills that we could have cured, our charity in saying to the poor, God will help you!

To be sure, a simpler style can be adopted on the stage, and the tone of the theatre can be reconciled in the drama with that of the world. But in this way, morals [manners] are not corrected; they are depicted, and an ugly face does not appear ugly to him who wears it. If we wish to correct them by caricaturing them, we leave the realm of probability and nature, and the picture no longer produces an effect. Caricature does not render objects hateful; it only renders them ridiculous. And out of this arises a very great difficulty; afraid of being ridiculous, men are no longer afraid of being vicious. The former cannot be remedied without promoting the latter. Why, you will ask, must I suppose this to be a necessary opposition? Why, Sir? Because the good do not make evil men objects of derision, but crush them with their contempt, and nothing is less funny or laughable than virtue's indignation. Ridicule, on the other hand, is the favorite arm of vice. With it, the respect that the heart owes to virtue is attacked at its root, and the love that is felt for it is finally extinguished.

Thus everything compels us to abandon this vain idea that some wish to give us of the perfection of a form of theatre directed toward public utility. It is an error, said the grave Muralt,[24] to hope that the true relations of things will be faithfully presented in the theatre. For, in general, the poet can only alter these relations in order to accommodate them to the taste of the public. In the comic, he diminishes them and sets them beneath man; in the tragic, he extends them to render them heroic and sets them above humanity. Thus they are never to his measure, and we always see beings other than our own kind in the theatre. I add that this difference is so true and so well recognized that Aristotle makes a rule of it in his poetics: *Comoedia enim deteriores, Tragoedia meliores quam nunc sont imitari conantur.*[25] Here is a well-conceived imitation, which proposes for its object that which does not exist at all and leaves, between defect and excess, that which is as a useless thing! But of what importance is the truth of the imitation, provided the illusion is there? The only object is to excite the curiosity of the public. These productions of wit and craft, like most others, have for their end only applause. When the author receives it and the actors share in it, the play has reached its goal, and no other advantage is sought. Now, if the benefit is non-existent, the harm remains; and since the latter is indisputable, the issue seems to me to be settled. But let us turn to some examples which will make the solution clearer.

III

I BELIEVE I can assert as a truth easy to prove, on the basis of those mentioned above, that the French theatre, with all of its faults, is nevertheless pretty nearly as perfect as it can be, whether from the point of view of pleasure or that of utility, and that these two advantages are in a relation that cannot be disturbed without taking from one more than would be given the other, which would make the theatre even less perfect. This is not to say that a man of genius could not invent a kind of play preferable to those which are established. But this new kind, needing the talents of the author to sustain itself, will necessarily die with him. And his successors, lacking the same resources, will always be forced to return to the common means of interesting and of pleasing. What are these means in our theatre? Celebrated actions, great names, great virtues, in tragedy; comic situations and the amusing in comedy; and always love in both.* I ask in what way morals [manners] can profit from all this?

I will be told that in these plays crime is always punished and virtue always rewarded. I answer that, even if this were so, most tragic actions are only pure fables, events known to be inventions of the poet, and so do not make a strong impression on the audience; as a result of showing them that we want to instruct them, we no longer instruct them. I answer, moreover, that these punishments and rewards are always effected by such extraordinary means that nothing similar is expected in the natural course of human things. Finally, I answer by denying the fact. It is not, nor can it be, generally true. For, since this end is not the one toward which authors direct their plays, they are likely to attain it rarely; and often it would be an obstacle to success. Vice or virtue?—what is the difference, provided that the public is overawed by an impression of greatness? So the French stage, undeniably the most perfect, or at least, the most correct which has ever existed, is no less the triumph of the great villains than of the most illustrious heroes: witness Catalina, Mahomet, Atreus[26] and many others.

I am well aware that one must not look to the catastrophe to judge the moral effect of a tragedy and that, in this respect, the

* The Greeks did not need to found the principal interest of their tragedy on love and actually did not do so. Our tragedy does not have the same resources and could not do without this interest. The reason for this difference will be seen in what follows.

end is fulfilled when the virtuous unfortunate is the object of more concern than the happy guilty party! This does not prevent the pretended rule from being violated in such a case. As there is no one who would not prefer to be Britannicus than Nero, I agree that we ought to consider the play which puts them on the stage to be a good one in this respect, even though Britannicus perishes in it. But, according to the same principle, what judgment must we bring to a tragedy in which, although the criminals are punished, they are presented to us in so favorable a light that our sympathies are entirely with them? Where Cato, the greatest of humans, plays the role of a pedant; where Cicero, the savior of the republic—Cicero, who of all those who have borne the name of fathers of their country was the first to have it and the only one to merit it—is shown as a vile orator, a coward; while the infamous Catalina, covered with crimes that we would not dare to mention, ready to slay all his magistrates and to reduce his country to ashes, has the role of a great man and gains by his talents, his firmness, and his courage all the esteem of the audience? For all that he may have had a strong character, if you please, was he any the less for that a hateful villain? And was it necessary to lend to the crimes of a brigand the coloring of a hero's exploits? To what else does the moral of such a play lead if not to the encouragement of Catalinas and to the bestowing on clever knaves of the benefits of the public esteem owed to the virtuous? But such is the taste that must be flattered on the stage; such are the morals [manners] of an educated age. Knowledge, wit, and courage alone have our admiration. And thou, modest Virtue, thou remain'st ever unhonored! Blind men that we are, amidst so much enlightenment! Victims of our own mad applause, will we never learn how much contempt and hate are deserved by any man who abuses the genius and the talent that nature gave him, to the hurt of humankind?

Atrée and *Mahomet* do not even use the feeble device of a final catastrophe. The monster who serves as hero in each of these two plays comfortably finishes his crimes and enjoys their benefits;

one of the two states the matter, in fitting terms, in the last verse of the tragedy:

> Finally I harvest the fruits of my crimes.[27]

I am prepared to believe that the audience, sent home with this fine maxim, will not conclude that crime pays in pleasure and enjoyment. But I ask, what will the play in which this maxim is set up as an example have profited them?

As for *Mahomet*, the fault of attaching the public admiration to the guilty party, who is really worthy of exactly the opposite, would be even greater if the author had not taken care to bring attention and veneration to a second character in such a way as to remove, or at least to balance, the terror and amazement which Mahomet inspires. Above all, the scene they have together is conducted with so much art that Mahomet, without being out of character, without losing any of the superiority belonging to him, is nevertheless eclipsed by the simple common sense and intrepid virtue of Zopire.* To dare to put two such interlocutors face to face, an author was needed who was well aware of his powers. I have never heard spoken all the praise of which this scene, in particular, seems to me to be worthy; but I do not know another in the French theatre where the hand of a master is more visibly imprinted, and where the sacred character of virtue more visibly triumphs over the elevation of genius.

Another consideration which tends to justify this play is that

* I remember having found more warmth and elevation in Omar in his relations with Zopire than in Mahomet himself; and I took this for a fault. In thinking it over, I changed my mind. Omar, carried away by his fanaticism, ought to speak of his master only with that transport of zeal and admiration which raises him above humanity. But Mahomet is not a fanatic; he is an impostor who, knowing that there is no question of playing the inspired prophet with Zopire, seeks to win him with an affected tone of confidence and through ambitious motives. This reasonable posture renders him necessarily less brilliant than Omar; he is so by the very fact that he is greater and is better able to judge men. He himself says this or makes it understood throughout the scene. It was hence my fault if I did not recognize this; but that is what happens to us little authors. In wishing to censure the writings of our masters, our thoughtlessness causes us to pick out a thousand faults which are beauties for men of judgment.

its purpose is not only to expose crimes but, in particular, the crimes of fanaticism, for the sake of teaching the people to understand it and to defend themselves against it. Unhappily, such efforts are quite useless and are not always without danger. Fanaticism is not an error, but a blind and stupid fury that reason can never confine. The only secret for preventing it from coming to birth is to restrain those who excite it. You can very well demonstrate to madmen that their chiefs are fooling them; they are no less fervent in following them. Once fanaticism exists, I see only one way left to stop its progress; that is to use its own arms against it. It has nothing to do with reasoning or convincing. One must leave philosophy behind, close the books, take the sword, and punish the impostors. What is more, I fear, with regard to Mahomet, that his greatness of soul diminishes the atrocity of his crimes by a great deal in the eyes of the spectators, and that such a play, given before people capable of choosing, would create more Mahomets than Zopires. At least, it is quite certain that such examples are not at all encouraging for virtue.

The black Atreus has none of these excuses; the horror which he inspires is a pure loss. He teaches us nothing other than to shudder at his crime; and, although he is great only in his rage, there is no other figure in the whole play who is capable, by his character, of sharing the public's attention with him. For, as to the mawkish Plisthenes, I do not know how he can be endured in such a tragedy. Seneca put no love in his; and since the modern author was able to bring himself to follow Seneca in all the rest, he would have done well to have imitated him in this too. Indeed, one must have a very flexible heart to tolerate amorous conversations along with Atreus' scenes.

Before finishing with this play, I cannot refrain from mentioning a merit in it which will, perhaps, seem to be a fault to many people. The role of Thyestes is, perhaps of all that have ever been put on our stage, the one that most approaches the taste of the ancients. He is not a courageous hero; he is not a model of virtue; it

could not be said, either, that he is a criminal.* He is a weak man
and nevertheless involves our sympathy on this basis alone: he is
a man and unfortunate. It seems, also, on this basis alone, that the
feeling which he inspires is extremely tender and moving. For this
man is very close to each of us; heroism, on the other hand, overwhelms us even more than it moves us, because, after all, what has
it to do with us? Would it not be desirable if our sublime authors
deigned to descend a little from their customary great heights and
touched us sometimes with simple suffering humanity, for fear
that having pity only for unhappy heroes we shall pity no one?
The ancients had heroes and put men on their stages; we, on the
contrary, put only heroes on the stage and hardly have any men.
The ancients spoke of humanity in less-studied phrases, but they
knew how to exercise it better. A story that Plutarch tells fits them
and us, and I cannot refrain from transcribing it. An old Athenian
was looking for a seat at the theatre and could not find one. Some
youngsters, seeing him in difficulty, waved to him from afar. He
came, but they pushed close together and made fun of him. The
good man made his way around the theatre in this fashion, not
knowing what to do with himself and constantly jeered by the
fair youth. The ambassadors of Sparta noticed it and, standing up
immediately, gave the old man an honorable place in their midst.
This action was observed by the whole audience and universally
applauded. "Woe is me," cried out the old man in a pained tone,
"the Athenians know what is decent, but the Lacedaemonians
practice it."[28] Here are modern philosophy and ancient morals
[manners].

I return to my subject. What do we learn from *Phèdre* and
Œdipe other than that man is not free and that heaven punishes
him for crimes that it makes him commit? What do we learn in
Médée other than how cruel and unnatural a mother can be made

* The proof of this is that he attracts us. As to the fault for which he is
punished, it is old, it is quite enough atoned for, and finally, it is a small thing
for a villain in the theatre; a villain in the theatre is not understood to be such
if he does not cause us to shudder in horror.

by the rage of jealousy? Look at most of the plays in the French theatre; in practically all of them you will find abominable monsters and atrocious actions, useful, if you please, in making the plays interesting and in giving exercise to the virtues; but they are certainly dangerous in that they accustom the eyes of the people to horrors that they ought not even to know and to crimes they ought not to suppose possible. It is not even true that murder and parricide are always hateful in the theatre. With the help of some easy suppositions, they are rendered permissible or pardonable. It is hard not to excuse Phaedra, who is incestuous and spills innocent blood. Syphax poisoning his wife, the young Horatius stabbing his sister, Agamemnon sacrificing his daughter, Orestes cutting his mother's throat, do not fail to be figures who arouse sympathy. Add that the author, in order to make each speak according to his character, is forced to put into the mouths of villains their maxims and principles clad in the magnificence of beautiful verse and recited in an imposing and sententious tone for the instruction of the audience.[29]

If the Greeks tolerated such theatre it was because it represented for them national traditions which were always common among the people, which they had reasons to recall constantly; and even its hateful aspects were part of its intention. Deprived of the same motives and the same concern, how can the same tragedy find, in your country, spectators capable of enduring the depictions it presents to them and the characters which are given life in it? One kills his father, marries his mother, and finds himself the brother of his children; another forces a son to slay his father; a third makes a father drink the blood of his son. We shudder at the very idea of the horrors with which the French stage is decked out for the amusement of the gentlest and the most humane people on earth! No . . . I maintain, and I bring in witness the terror of my readers, that the massacres of the gladiators were not so barbarous as these frightful plays. At the circus one saw blood flowing, it is true; but one did not soil his imagination with crimes at which nature trembles.

IV

HAPPILY, the tragedy such as it exists is so far from us, it presents beings so enormous, so bloated, so chimerical, that the example of their vices is hardly more contagious than that of their virtues is useful; and, to the extent it wants to instruct us less, it does us also less harm. But it is not so with comedy, the morals [manners] of which have a more immediate relationship with ours, and whose characters resemble men more. It is all bad and pernicious; every aspect strikes home with the audience. And since the very pleasure of the comic is founded on a vice of the human heart, it is a consequence of this principle that the more the comedy is amusing and perfect, the more its effect is disastrous for morals [manners]. But, without repeating what I have already said of its nature, I shall limit myself here to applying it and shall take a look at your comic theatre.

Take it in its perfection, that is to say, at its birth. It is agreed, and it is more clearly grasped every day, that Molière is the most perfect comic author whose works are known to us. But who can deny also that the theatre of this same Molière, of whose talents I am a greater admirer than anyone, is a school of vices and bad morals [manners] even more dangerous than the very books which profess to teach them? His greatest care is to ridicule goodness and simplicity and to present treachery and falsehood so that they arouse our interest and sympathy. His decent people only talk; his vicious characters act, and the most brilliant successes accompany them most of the time. Finally, the honor of applause is reserved rarely for those who are the most respectable, and goes almost always to the cleverest.

Consider what is comic in this author. Everywhere you will

find that the vices of character are its instrument, and the natural failings its subject; that the malice of the former punishes the simplicity of the latter; and that fools are the victims of the vicious. Because this is only too true in the world does not mean that it should be put on the stage with an air of approval, as if to excite perfidious souls to punish, under the name of folly, the candor of decent men:

Dat veniam corvis, vexat censura columbas.[30]

This is the general spirit of Molière and his imitators. They are men who, at the most, sometimes make fun of the vices without ever making virtue loved—men who, as one of the ancients said, know how to snuff out the lamp but who never put any oil in it.

See how this man, for the sake of multiplying his jokes, shakes the whole order of society; how scandalously he overturns all the most sacred relations on which it is founded; how ridiculous he makes the respectable rights of fathers over their children, of husbands over their wives, of masters over their servants! He makes us laugh, it is true, and for that he is all the more guilty, in forcing, by an invincible charm, even the wise to lend themselves to jests which ought to call forth their indignation. I hear it said that he attacks the vices; but I should like those that he attacks to be compared with those he encourages. Who is more blameworthy, the unintelligent man of the middle class who foolishly plays the gentleman, or the rascally gentleman who dupes him? In the play of which I speak,[31] is it not the latter who is the decent man? Is not the sympathy on his side, and does not the public applaud him at every trick he plays on the other? Who is the more criminal, a peasant so mad as to marry a lady, or a wife who seeks to dishonor her husband? What is to be thought of a play at which the audience applauds the infidelity, the lying, and impudence of the latter and laughs at the stupidity of the dolt punished?[32] It is a great vice to be miserly and to loan usuriously; but is it not even a greater one for a son to rob his father, to lack respect for him, to make him a thousand insulting reproaches and, when the father, vexed, gives the son his malediction, to answer with a sneer that he does not know what to do with his father's gifts? If the joke is excellent, is it any the less punishable? And is the play which makes the insolent son who did this liked any the less a school of bad morals [manners]?[33]

I shall not stop to speak of valets. They are condemned by everyone;* and it would be all the more unjust to impute to Molière the errors of his models and of his age, since he emancipated himself from them. We shall not take advantage of the ineptitudes which might be found in the works of his youth or of what is less good in his other plays, but will go directly to what is universally recognized to be his masterpiece; I mean the *Misanthrope*.

I find that this comedy reveals better than any other the true aims for which Molière composed his theatre, and through it we can better judge its real effects. Since he had to please the public, he consulted the most general taste of those who constitute it; according to this taste he formed a model, and according to this model he drew a picture of the contrary failings from which he took his comic characteristics, various features of which he distributed in his plays. He did not, then, pretend to form a good man but a man of the world. Consequently, he did not wish to correct the vices, but what is ridiculous. And, as I have already said, he found in vice itself a fitting instrument to accomplish this. Thus, wishing to expose to public derision all the failings opposed to the qualities of the likable man—the man of society—after he had played so many other ridiculous characters, there remained to him that one which the world pardons the least, the one who is ridiculous because he is virtuous. This is what he did in the *Misanthrope*.

You could not deny me two things: one, that Alceste in this play is a righteous man, sincere, worthy, truly a good man; and, second,

* I do not decide if one actually ought to condemn them. It is possible that valets are only the instruments of their master's viciousness, since the masters have taken the honor of invention away from them. However, I suspect that the somewhat too naive image of society is good for the theatre in this case. Supposing that some knavery is necessary in plays, I do not know if it is not better that the valets be responsible for it and that the decent folk be left as decent folk: at least on the stage.

that the author makes him a ridiculous figure. This is already enough, it seems to me, to render Molière inexcusable. It could be said that he played in Alceste not virtue but a true failing—the hatred of men. To that I answer that it is not true that he gave this hatred to his character. This name, misanthrope, must not give the false impression that the one who bears it is the enemy of mankind. Such a hatred would not be a failing but a perversion of nature, and the greatest of all vices. Since all the social virtues relate back to beneficence, nothing is so directly contrary to them as inhumanity.[34] The true misanthrope is a monster. If he could exist, he would not cause laughter but horror. You may have seen in the Italian theatre a play entitled *la Vie est un songe*.[35] If you recall the hero, there you have the real misanthrope.

Who, then, is the misanthrope of Molière? A good man who detests the morals [manners] of his age and the viciousness of his contemporaries; who, precisely because he loves his fellow creatures, hates in them the evils they do to one another and the vices of which these evils are the product. If he were less touched by the errors of humanity, if he suffered less from indignation at the iniquities he sees, would he be more humane himself? It would be as well to assert that a tender father loves another's children more than his own because he is angered by the faults of his own and never says anything to the children of others.

These sentiments of the misanthrope are perfectly developed in his role. He says, I admit, that he has conceived a terrible hatred of humankind. But on what occasion does he say it?* When, outraged at having seen his friend betray his sentiments like a coward and deceive the man who asked him for them, he sees that at the peak of his anger he is being made fun of to boot. It is natural that

* I warn my readers that, since I am without books, without memory, and without any materials other than a confused reminiscence of the observations that I have made in the theatre in the past, I may cite erroneously and confuse the order of the plays. But if my examples are not very adequate, my reasons will nonetheless be so inasmuch as they are not drawn from one play or the other but from the general spirit of the theatre, which I have studied well.

this anger should degenerate into fury and make him then say what he would not think when composed. Besides, the reason he gives for this universal hate fully justifies his cause:

> *Some because they are vicious,*
> *The others for being obliging to the vicious.*

Hence, it is not of men that he is the enemy, but of the viciousness of some and of the support this viciousness finds in the others. If there were neither knaves nor flatterers, he would love all humankind. There is no good man who is not a misanthrope in this sense; or, rather, the real misanthropes are those who do not think as he does. For, in the final accounting, I know of no greater enemy of man than everybody's friend who, always charmed by everything, constantly encourages the vicious, and who, by his culpable complacency, flatters the vices out of which are born all the disorders of society.

A certain proof that Alceste is not literally a misanthrope is that, even with his bluntness and insults, he does not fail to arouse sympathy or to please. The audience would certainly not want to be like him, because so much righteousness is very uncomfortable; but not one of them would find it disagreeable to have to do with someone who resembled him; this could not happen if he were the declared enemy of men. In all the other plays of Molière, the ridiculous character is always detestable or contemptible. In this one, although Alceste has real failings at which it would not be wrong to laugh, one cannot help feeling respect for him deep in one's heart. On this occasion the force of virtue wins out over the art of the author and does honor to his character. Although Molière wrote reprehensible plays, he was personally a decent man; and the brush of a decent man has never been able to paint the features of righteousness and probity with odious colors. What is more, Molière put into Alceste's mouth so great a number of his own maxims that many have thought that he wanted to depict himself. This appeared in the resentment felt in the audience at the

first performance when they found they did not share the misanthrope's opinion about the sonnet;[36] for it was evident that it was
the author's own.

Nevertheless, this virtuous character is presented as ridiculous.
It is indeed ridiculous in certain respects, and what demonstrates
that the poet's intention is really to make it so is Philinte's character, which he sets in opposition to the other. This Philinte is the
wise man of the play: one of those decent members of high society
whose maxims resemble so much those of knaves, one of those
gentle, moderate people who always find that everything is fine
because it is to their interest that nothing be better, who are always
satisfied with everyone because they do not care about anyone;
who, at a good dinner, assert that it is not true that the people are
hungry; who, with a well-lined pocket, find it quite disagreeable
that some declaim in favor of the poor; who, their own doors well
secured, would see the whole of humankind robbed, plundered,
slain, and massacred without complaining, given that God has
endowed them with a most meritorious gentleness with which they
are able to support the misfortunes of others.

It is clear that the reasoning apathy of this figure is quite suitable for intensifying and setting off in a comic fashion the furies of
the other. And the fault of Molière is not that he made the misanthrope an irritable and bilious man, but that he gave him childish
rages about subjects that ought not to have touched him. The
character of the misanthrope is not at the poet's disposal; it is determined by the nature of his dominant passion. This passion is a
violent hatred of vice, born from an ardent love of virtue and
soured by the continual spectacle of men's viciousness. It is, then,
only a great and noble soul which is susceptible to it. The horror
and contempt which this same passion nourishes for all the vices
which have vexed it, serves also to keep these vices from the heart
it agitates. Further, this continual contemplation of the disorders
of society detaches him from himself and fixes all his attention on
humankind. This habit raises and enlarges his ideas and destroys in

him the base inclinations which nourish and strengthen vanity, and out of this conjuncture of effects is born a certain courageous force, a pride of character which leaves room in his soul only for sentiments worthy of occupying it.

This is not to say that man is not ever man, that passion does not often render him weak, unjust, and unreasonable; that he does not perhaps spy out the hidden motives of others' action with a secret pleasure at finding the corruption of their hearts; that a small wrong does not often make him very wrathful; and that in irritating him purposefully a clever villain cannot succeed in making him appear to be a villain himself. But it is nonetheless true that not all means are good for producing these effects, and that they must be fitted to the misanthrope's character in order to put it into motion; otherwise, one substitutes another man for the misanthrope and paints him with other features than his own.

This, then, is the way in which the misanthrope's character ought to show its failings, and this is also what Molière makes use of admirably in all of Alceste's scenes with his friend, where the cold maxims and the jests of the latter constantly deflate him and make him say countless well-timed absurdities. But this hard and unbending character, which at moments gives him so much gall and sourness, removes him at the same time from every puerile chagrin that has no reasonable basis and from every intense personal interest to which he ought not to be susceptible. Let him be enraged at every disorder at which he is only a witness, for this is only one more detail in the picture; but make him cold in what directly concerns himself. For, having declared war on the vicious, he must expect that they in turn will declare it on him. If he had not foreseen the harm that his frankness would do him, it would be a folly and not a virtue. If a false woman betray him, unworthy friends dishonor him, or weak friends abandon him, he must suffer it without a murmur. He knows men.

If these distinctions are correct, Molière has misunderstood the misanthrope. Can it be thought that he did it unawares? Certainly not. This is how the desire to cause laughter at the expense of the character forced him to degrade it contrary to its truth.

After the adventure of the sonnet, how could Alceste not expect the bad turns of Oronte? Could he be astonished when he learns of them, as if it were the first time in his life that he had been sincere, or the first time that his sincerity had made an enemy? Ought he not, rather, prepare himself quietly for the loss of his case than give evidence of a childish spite beforehand?

> *This can well cost me twenty thousand francs;*
> *But for twenty thousand francs I shall have*
> *the right to storm.*

A misanthrope need not buy the right to storm so dearly; he has only to open his eyes; he does not care for money enough to believe that, because he has lost a trial, he has acquired a new right on this point. But one had to make the audience laugh.

In the scene with Du Bois, the more Alceste has cause to become impatient, the more he ought to remain phlegmatic and cold, because the silliness of the valet is not a vice. The misanthrope and the man in a fury are two very different characters. This was an occasion upon which to distinguish them. Molière was not unaware of it; but he had to make the audience laugh.

At the risk of making the reader laugh too, at my expense, I dare to accuse this author of having missed an opportunity for greater harmony, for greater truthfulness, and perhaps for new beauties of situation. He could have made a change in his plan so that Philinte entered as a necessary actor into the plot of the play, putting his actions and those of Alceste in apparent opposition with their principles and in perfect conformity with their characters. I mean that the misanthrope should have always been furious against public vices and always tranquil about the personal viciousness of which he was the victim. On the other hand, the philosopher Philinte ought to have seen all the disorders of society with a stoical phlegm and set himself in a fury at the slightest harm directed personally to himself. Actually, I notice that these people who are

so easy-going about public injustices are always those who make
the most noise at the least injury done them, and that they stand by
their philosophy only so long as they have no need of it for themselves. They resemble that Irishman who did not want to get out of
bed although the house was on fire. "The house is burning," they
yelled to him. "What difference does it make to me?" he answered,
"I am only renting it." Finally, the fire reached him. Immediately,
he bounded out, ran, screamed, and became disturbed. He began
to understand that sometimes we must take an interest in the house
in which we live even though it does not belong to us.

It seems to me that, in treating the characters in question along
these lines, each of them would have been truer, more theatrical,
and that Alceste would have been incomparably more effective.
But then the audience could only have laughed at the expense
of the man of the world, and the author's intention was that they
laugh at the expense of the misanthrope.* With the same
intent, he sometimes gives Alceste lines expressing a bad temper
entirely contrary to the taste with which he endowed him. Such is
the pun from the sonnet scene:

> *A plague on thy Fall, Devil's poisoner!*
> *May thou have a fall to break thy nose.*

This is a pun so much the more out of place in the misanthrope's
mouth, since he has just criticized more bearable ones in Oronte's
sonnet. And it is very curious that, a moment later, he who com-
poses it proposes the *Chanson du roi Henri* as a model of taste. It is
useless to maintain that this line escapes in a moment of spite; for
spite can dictate nothing less than puns, and Alceste, who spends

---

* I do not doubt that, on the basis of the idea that I have just proposed, a
man of genius could compose a new *Misanthrope*, not less true nor less natural
than the Athenian one, equal in merit to that of Molière and incomparably
more instructive. I see only one difficulty for this new play, which is that it
could not succeed. For, whatever one may say, in things that dishonor, no
one laughs with good grace at his own expense. Here we are caught up again
in my principles.

his life scolding, ought, even in scolding, to have taken a tone more appropriate to his turn of mind:

Good lord! Vile flatterer! You praise follies.

This is the way the misanthrope ought to speak in anger. Never will a pun go well after that. But one had to make the audience laugh; and it is thus that one abases virtue.

A rather notable aspect of this comedy is that the foreign features which the author gave to the misanthrope's role forced him to dilute what was essential to the character. Thus, while in all his other plays the characters are heightened to make the greatest effect, in this one the traits are blunted to render it more theatrical. The same scene about which I have just spoken provides me with the proof. In it, Alceste is seen to be evasive and roundabout in giving his opinion to Oronte. This is not at all the misanthrope. It is a decent man of the world who takes great pains to fool the man who consults him. The force of the character insists that he say bluntly, "Your sonnet is worthless; throw it in the fire." But that would have taken away the humor born of the misanthrope's perplexity and of his repetitions of "I don't say that," which, nevertheless, are really only falsehoods. If Philinte, following his example, had said at this point, "And what do you say now, deceiver?" what could Alceste answer? In truth, it is not worth continuing to be a misanthrope when he is one only halfway. For if one permits oneself the first circumspection and the first alteration of the truth, where is the sufficient reason for stopping before one becomes as false as a courtier?

Alceste's friend ought to know him. How can he dare propose to him that they go to see the judges, that is to say, in honest terms, that they seek to corrupt them? How can he suppose that a man capable of renouncing even propriety for the love of virtue could be capable of neglecting his duties for private interest? Solicit a judge; one need not be a misanthrope—it suffices to be a decent man—to have no part of it. For, whatever face one puts on the thing, either the one who solicits a judge exhorts him to do his duty and hence insults him; or he proposes that he take persons into consideration and hence wants to seduce him, since any consideration of persons is a crime for a judge, who ought to consider the suit and not its parties and ought to look only to order and the law. Now, I say that to engage a judge to do a bad action is to do one oneself, and that it is better to lose a just cause than to do a bad action. That is clear and evident; there is nothing to answer to it. Worldly morality has different maxims; I am not unaware of that. It is enough for me that I show that in everything which made the misanthrope so ridiculous he was only doing the duty of a good man, and that his character was badly developed from the beginning if his friend supposed that he could fail in his duty.

If this skilful author sometimes lets this character act with all its force, it is only when this force renders the scene more theatrical and produces a more perceptible comedy of contrasts or situation. Such is, for example, the taciturn and silent temper of Alceste, and then the intrepid and vigorously punctuated censure in the conversation at the coquette's.

All right, steady, thrust, my good friends of the court.

Here the author has strongly accentuated the distinction between the slanderer and the misanthrope. The latter, with his sharp and biting spleen, abhors calumny and detests satire. It is public vices and the vicious in general that he attacks. Low and secret slander is unworthy of him; he despises it and hates it in others. And, when he has something bad to say of someone, he begins by saying it to his face. Thus nowhere else in the entire play is he as effective as in this scene, because it is here that he is what he ought to be; and if he makes the audience laugh, decent men do not blush for having laughed.

But, in general, it cannot be denied that if the misanthrope were more of a misanthrope he would be a great deal less funny; for his frankness and firmness, never permitting him to be roundabout, would never leave him at a loss. It is not then out of consideration for him that the author sometimes dilutes his character;

it is, on the contrary, to make him more ridiculous. Yet, another reason forces Molière to it; the misanthrope in the theatre, having to speak about what he sees, must live in society and, consequently, must temper his righteousness and his ways by some of those lying and false considerations of which politeness consists and which society exacts from whomever wants to be tolerated in it. If he acted otherwise, his words would have no effect at all. It is the author's interest to make him ridiculous but not mad; and that is how he would appear to the eyes of the public if he were entirely wise.

It is difficult to leave this admirable play when one has begun to treat it; and the more one thinks about it, the more one finds new beauties in it. But, finally, since it is, of all Molière's comedies, indisputably the one which contains the best and healthiest moral, from it we can judge the others. And let us agree that, since the intention of the author is to please corrupt minds, either his morality leads to evil, or the false good that he preaches is more dangerous than the evil itself: in that it seduces by an appearance of reason; in that it causes the practice and the principles of society to be preferred to exact probity; in that it makes wisdom consist in a certain mean between vice and virtue; in that, to the great relief of the audience, it persuades them that to be a decent man it suffices not to be a complete villain.

I would be at too great an advantage if I wanted to turn, after the consideration of Molière, to that of his successors, who, without his genius and probity, followed, all the better for that, his interested views in dedicating themselves to flattering debauched young men and women without morals [manners].[37] I will not do Dancourt the honor of speaking of him. His plays do not shock with obscene words, but, to tolerate them, only one's ears can be chaste. Regnard, more modest, is no less dangerous; leaving the other to amuse fallen women, he undertakes the formation of cheats. It is unbelievable that, with the accord of the police,[38] a comedy is publicly played right in Paris in which a nephew, the hero of the play, along with his worthy attendants, in the apartment of his uncle whom he has just witnessed dying, busies himself with activities which the law punishes with the rope; and that, instead of shedding the tears which simple humanity elicits from even the indifferent under such circumstances, they vie with one another to lighten the sad rites of death with barbarous jokes. The most sacred rights, the most touching sentiments of nature, are played upon in this dreadful scene. The most criminal acts are wantonly gathered together here with a playfulness which makes all this pass for nicety. Counterfeiting, forgery, theft, imposture, lying, cruelty; everything is there, everything is applauded. When the dead man takes it into his head to rise again, to the great displeasure of his dear nephew, and is not willing to ratify what has been done in his name, the means are found to extract his consent by force, and everything comes out to the satisfaction of the actors and the spectators. In spite of themselves, the latter have identified with these wretches and leave the play with the edifying reminiscence of having been, in the depths of their hearts, accomplices of the crimes they have seen committed.[39]

Let us dare to say it without being roundabout. Which of us is sure enough of himself to bear the performance of such a comedy without halfway taking part in the deeds which are played in it? Who would not be a bit distressed if the thief were to be taken by surprise or fail in his attempt? Who does not himself become a thief for a minute in being concerned about him? For is being concerned about someone anything other than putting oneself in his place? A fine instruction for the youth, one in which grown men have difficulty protecting themselves from the seductions of vice! Is that to say that it is never permissible to show blamable actions in the theatre? No; but, in truth, to know how to put a rascal on the stage, a very good man must be the author.

These failings are so inherent to our theatre that, in wanting to remove them, it is disfigured. Our contemporary authors, guided by the best of intentions, write more refined plays. But what happens then? They are no longer really comic and produce no effect.

They are very instructive, if you please; but they are even more boring. One might as well go to a sermon.

V

In this decadence of the theatre, we are constrained to substitute for the true beauties, now eclipsed, little pleasurable accessories capable of impressing the multitude. No longer able to maintain the strength of comic situations and character, the love interest has been reinforced. The same has been done in tragedy to take the place of situations drawn from political concerns we no longer have, and of simple and natural sentiments which no longer move anyone. The authors, in the public interest, contest with one another to give a new energy and a new coloring to this dangerous passion; and, since Molière and Corneille, only romances, under the name of dramatic plays, succeed in the theatre.

Love is the realm of women. It is they who necessarily give the law in it, because, according to the order of nature, resistance belongs to them, and men can conquer this resistance only at the expense of their liberty. Hence, a natural effect of this sort of play is to extend the empire of the fair sex, to make women and girls the preceptors of the public, and to give them the same power over the audience that they have over their lovers. Do you think, Sir, that this order is without its difficulties; and that, in taking so much effort to increase the ascendancy of women, men will be the better governed for it?

It is possible that there are in the world a few women worthy of being listened to by a serious man; but, in general, is it from women that he ought to take counsel, and is there no way of honoring their sex without abasing our own? Nature's most charming object, the one most able to touch a sensitive heart and to lead it to the good, is, I admit, an agreeable and virtuous woman. But where is this celestial object hiding itself? Is it not cruel to contemplate it with so much pleasure in the theatre, only to find such a different sort in society? Nevertheless, the seductive picture makes its effect. The enchantment produced by these prodigies of prudence is turned to the profit of women without honor. If a young man has seen the world only on the stage, the first way to approach virtue which presents itself to him is to look for a mistress who will lead him there, hoping of course to find a Constance or a Cénie,* at the very least.[40] It is thus, on the faith in an imaginary model, on a modest and moving manner, on a counterfeited sweetness, *nescius aurae fallacis*,[41] that the young fool goes to his destruction thinking he is becoming wise.

This gives me the occasion to pose a sort of problem. The ancients had, in general, a very great respect for women;** but they showed this respect by refraining from exposing them to public judgment, and thought to honor their modesty by keeping quiet about their other virtues. They had as their maxim that the land where morals [manners] were purest was the one where they spoke the least of women, and that the best woman was the one about whom the least was said. It is on this principle that a Spartan, hearing a foreigner singing the praises of a lady of his acquaintance, interrupted him in anger: "Won't you stop," he said to him, "slandering a virtuous woman?"[43] From this also came the fact that in their drama the only roles representing women in love and mar-

---

* It is not out of thoughtlessness that I cite Cénie here, although this charming play is the work of a woman. For, seeking the truth in good faith, I cannot disguise what happens contrary to my opinion. And it is not to a woman that I refuse the talents of men, but to women. I am all the more willing to praise the talents of the author of *Cénie* in particular, because I have suffered from her words and can thus render her a pure and disinterested homage, as are all those issued from my pen.

** They gave them many honorable names which we have no more or which are low and outdated for us. It is well known what use Virgil made of the name *Matres* on an occasion when the Trojan mothers were not very prudent.[42] We have in their place only the word *ladies* (*Dames*) which is not suitable for all, which is even gradually becoming antiquated, and has been completely banished from elegant usage. I observe that the ancients drew their titles of honor preferably from the rights of nature, while we draw ours only from the rights of rank.

riageable girls were of slaves or prostitutes. They had such an idea of the modesty of the fair sex that they would have thought they failed in the respect owed to it, if they even represented decent girls on the stage.* In a word, the image of open vice shocked them less than that of offended modesty.

With us, on the contrary, the most esteemed woman is the one who has the greatest renown, about whom the most is said, who is the most often seen in society, at whose home one dines the most, who most imperiously sets the tone, who judges, resolves, decides, pronounces, assigns talents, merit, and virtues their degrees and places, and whose favor is most ignominiously begged for by humble, learned men. On the stage it is even worse. Actually, in society they do not know anything, although they judge everything; but in the theatre, learned in the learning of men and philosophers, thanks to the authors, they crush our sex with its own talents, and the imbecile audiences go right ahead and learn from women what they took efforts to dictate to them. All of this, in truth, is to make fun of them, to tax them with a puerile vanity; and I do not doubt that the most prudent among them are indignant about it. Look through most contemporary plays; it is always a woman who knows everything, who teaches everything to men. It is always the court lady who makes the little Jean de Saintré[44] repeat his catechism. A child would not be able to eat his bread if it were not cut by his governess. This is the image of what goes on in our new plays. The maid is on the stage and the children in the audience. Once more, I do not deny that this method has its advantages and that such preceptors can give weight and value to their lessons. But let us return to my question. I ask, which is more honorable to women and best renders to their sex the true respects due it, the ancient way or ours?

The same cause which gives the ascendancy to women over

* If they did otherwise in tragedies, it is because, following the political system of their theatre, they were not distressed if it were believed that persons of a high rank have no need of modesty and are always exceptions to the rules of morality.

men in our tragic and comic plays gives it also to the young over
the old, and this is another perversion of natural relations which is
no less reprehensible. Since the concern is always for the lovers, it
follows that the older characters can only play subordinate roles.
Either, to form the problem of the plot, they serve as obstacles to
the wishes of the young lovers and are then detestable; or they are
themselves in love and are ridiculous. *Turpe senex miles.*[45] Older
people are tyrants and usurpers in tragedy; in comedies, they are
jealous men, moneylenders, pedants, and insufferable fathers whom
everybody conspires to fool. This is the honorable view given of
old age in the theatre; this is the respect for it with which the young
are inspired. Let us thank the illustrious author of *Zaïre* and *Nanine*
for having protected the venerable Luzignan and the good old
Philippe Humbert from this contempt. There are a few others too.
But do these suffice to stop the torrent of public prejudice and to
efface the degradation most authors delight in attaching to the age
of wisdom, experience, and authority? Who can doubt that the
habit of always seeing old persons in the theatre as odious characters helps them to be rejected in society, and that, in accustoming
us to confound those who are seen in society with the babblers and
dotards of comedy, they all end up being equally despised? Observe
in a group at Paris the satisfied and vain air, the firm and decisive
tone of an impudent younger generation, while the old, timid and
modest, either do not dare to open their mouths or are hardly
listened to. Is anything similar seen in the provinces and in the
places where the theatre is not established? And everywhere on
earth, outside of the big cities, do not a grey beard and white hair
always command respect? I will be told that in Paris the old contribute to making themselves contemptible by giving up the bearing which is appropriate to them and by indecently taking on the
costume and the ways of the young; and that, since they play gal-
lants after the fashion of youth, it is only natural that youth be
preferred to them in its own trade. But, all to the contrary, it is
because they have no other means to make themselves tolerated

that they are constrained to fall back on this one; and they prefer
to be tolerated for their absurdity rather than to be entirely banished. Assuredly, it is not that by playing at being attractive they
become so, or that a gallant sexagenarian is a very gracious per-
sonnage. But his very unseemliness turns to his profit. It is one more
triumph for a woman who, dragging a Nestor in her train, thinks
she proves thereby that glacial age is not proof against the flame
she inspires. That is why women encourage these deans of Citherea
as much as they can, and have the malice to treat as charming men,
old lunatics whom they would find less likeable if they were less
absurd. But, let us return to my subject.

These effects are not the only ones produced by a stage whose
sole interest is founded on love. Many others, graver and more
important, are attributed to it, the reality of which I shall not
examine here but which have often been powerfully alleged by the
ecclesiastical writers. They have been answered that the dangers a
depiction of a contagious passion can produce are guarded against
by the way it is presented. The love that is played in the theatre is
made legitimate; its end is decent; often, it is sacrificed to duty and
virtue; and, as soon as it is guilty, it is punished. Very well; but is it
not ridiculous to pretend that the motions of the heart can be
governed, after the event, according to the precepts of reason, and
that the results must be awaited to know what impression ought to
be made by the situations which lead to them? The harm for which
the theatre is reproached is not precisely that of inspiring criminal
passions but of disposing the soul to feelings which are too tender
and which are later satisfied at the expense of virtue. The sweet
emotions that are felt are not in themselves a definite object, but
they produce the need for one. They do not precisely cause love,
but they prepare the way for its being experienced. They do not
choose the person who ought to be loved, but they force us to make
this choice. Thus, they are innocent or criminal only from the use
that we make of them according to our character, and this character is independent of the example. Even if it were true that only

legitimate passions are painted in the theatre, does it follow that
the impressions are weaker, that the effects are less dangerous? As
if the lively images of an innocent tenderness were less sweet, less
seductive, less capable of inflaming a sensitive heart than those of a
criminal love to which at least the horror of vice serves as a counter-
poison? But, if the idea of innocence embellishes for a few moments
the sentiment that it accompanies, the circumstances are soon ef-
faced from the memory, while the impression of such a sweet passion remains engraved in the depths of the heart. When the pa-
trician Manilius was driven from the senate of Rome for having
kissed his wife in the presence of his daughter, considering this
action only in itself, what had he done that was reprehensible?[46]
Nothing, unquestionably; the kiss even gave expression to a laudable sentiment. But the chaste flames of the mother could inspire
impure ones in the daughter. Hence, an example for corruption
could be taken from a very decent action. This is the effect of the
theatre's permissible loves.

It is pretended that we can be cured of love by the depiction
of its weaknesses. I do not know how the authors go about it; but
I see that the spectators are always on the side of the weak lover
and that they are often distressed when he is not even weaker. I
ask if that is quite the way to avoid resembling him?

Recall, Sir, a play that I believe I remember seeing with you
some years ago and that gave us a pleasure we hardly expected,
whether the author put more theatrical beauties in it than we had
thought or whether the actress lent her wonted charm to the role,
which she brought to a fuller realization. I mean the *Bérénice* of
Racine. In what state of mind does the viewer see this play begin?
With a sentiment of contempt for an emperor and a Roman who
sways, like the lowest of men, between his mistress and his duty;
who, drifting incessantly in a shameful incertitude, debases by
effeminate complaints that almost divine character given him by
history, who makes us look for the benefactor of the world and
the delight of humankind in a vile salon wooer. What does the

same spectator think after the performance? He ends up pitying this sensitive man whom he despised, by being concerned with the same passion which he considered criminal, by secretly grumbling at the sacrifice he is forced to make for the laws of his country. This is what both of us experienced at the performance. The role of Titus, very well played, would have been effective if it had been up to the level of the man. But everyone felt that the principal concern was for Bérénice and that it was the fate of her love which determined the character of the catastrophe. Not that her continual complaints produced a great emotion during the course of the play; but, when in the fifth act, she ceased to complain, and with a bleak air, a dry eye, and a dull voice, gave expression to a cold misery approaching despair, the art of the actress combined with the pathos of the role; and the spectators, deeply moved, began to cry when Bérénice cried no more. What did this mean, if not that we feared that she would be sent away, that we felt beforehand the pain that would overwhelm her heart, and that everyone wanted Titus to let himself be overcome, even at the risk of respecting him less? Is this not a tragedy which has attained its object and which has taught the spectators to surmount the weaknesses of love?

The conclusion disappoints these secret wishes, but what difference does it make? The outcome does not erase the effect of the play. The queen departs without the leave of the audience. The Emperor sends her away *invitus invitam;* one might add, *invito spectatore.*[47] Titus can very well remain a Roman; he is the only one on his side; all the spectators have married Bérénice.

Even if this effect could be disputed; even if it be maintained that the example of force and virtue that is manifested in Titus, conqueror of himself, is the root of the play's appeal and makes it possible that in pitying Bérénice we are glad to do so, this would only go to prove my principles. This is because, as I have said, the sacrifices made to duty and virtue always have a secret charm, even for corrupted hearts; and the proof that this sentiment is not the work of the play is that they have it before it begins. But that does not prevent certain passions satisfied from seeming to them preferable to virtue itself; nor does it mean that, although content to see Titus virtuous and magnanimous, they would not be even more so if they saw him happy and weak, or, at least, that they would not readily agree to be so in his place. To render this truth palpable, imagine an outcome completely contrary to the author's. After having once again consulted his heart, Titus, wanting neither to violate Rome's laws nor to sell out his happiness to ambition, comes, with contrary maxims, to abdicate the throne at the feet of Bérénice; affected by such a great sacrifice, she feels it her duty to refuse the hand of her lover, but nevertheless accepts it. Both, intoxicated by the charms of love, peace, and innocence, renounce vain greatness and, with that sweet joy that the true impulses of nature inspire, choose to go and live, happy and neglected, in some corner of the earth. Let this touching scene be animated with the tender and moving sentiments which the subject furnishes and which Racine would have put to such effective use. Give Titus a speech addressed to the Romans on taking his leave of them that is appropriate to the circumstance and the subject; is it not clear that, unless the author is unusually clumsy, such a speech will make the whole assemblage dissolve in tears? The play, ending thus, will be, if you please, less good, less instructive, less conformable to history; but will it cause less pleasure, and will the spectators leave less satisfied? The first four acts would remain pretty much as they are; nevertheless, an entirely contrary lesson would be drawn from them. So true is it that the depictions of love always make a greater impression than the maxims of wisdom, and that the total effect of a tragedy is entirely independent of the effect of the outcome.*

Do you wish to know if it is certain that tragedy, in showing the fatal consequences of immoderate passions, teaches us to pro-

* In the seventh volume of *Pamela*[48] there is a very judicious study of Racine's *Andromache* from which it can be seen that this play attains its pretended goal no better than all the others.

tect ourselves against them? Consult your experience. These fatal consequences are very strongly represented in *Zaïre*. They cost the lives of the two lovers and far more than the life of Orosmane, since he takes his life only to deliver himself from the most painful sentiment that can touch a human heart: remorse for having stabbed his mistress. These are, assuredly, most forceful lessons. I should be interested to find someone, man or woman, who would dare to boast of having left a performance of *Zaïre* well-armed against love. As for me, I think I hear every spectator saying in his heart at the end of the tragedy: Ah, would that I were given a Zaïre; I should see to it that I should not have to kill her. If women themselves do not tire of flocking to this enchanting play, or of making men flock to it too, I cannot say that they do so to strengthen, by the heroine's example, their resolves not to imitate a sacrifice which turns out so badly for her; rather, of all the tragedies of the theatre, no other shows with more charm the power of love and the empire of beauty, and, as a premium, one is taught by it never to judge one's mistress by appearances. When Orosmane sacrifices Zaïre to his jealousy, a sensible woman looks on the transports of the passion without terror; for it is a lesser misfortune to perish by the hand of her lover than to be poorly loved by him.

However love is depicted for us, it seduces or it is not love. If it is badly depicted, the play is bad. If it is well depicted, it overshadows everything that accompanies it. Its combats, its troubles, its sufferings, make it still more touching than if it had no resistance to overcome. Far from its sad effects putting us off, love becomes only more appealing by its very misfortunes. We say, in spite of ourselves, that such a delicious sentiment makes up for everything. So sweet an image softens the heart without its being noticed. We take from the passion that part which leads to pleasure, and put aside that which torments. No one thinks he is obliged to be a hero; and it is thus that in admiring decent love one abandons oneself to criminal love.

What succeeds in making these images dangerous is precisely

what is done to make them agreeable; love never reigns on the stage other than in decent souls; the two lovers are always models of perfection. And how could one fail to be attracted by such a seductive passion between two hearts whose characters are already so attractive in themselves? I doubt whether in our entire drama one single play can be found in which mutual love does not have the favor of the spectator. If some unlucky fellow is inflamed by an unreciprocated passion, he becomes the butt of the audience. The poets think they are working wonders in making a lover estimable or detestable according to whether he is well or ill received in his loves, in making the public always approve the sentiments of his mistress, and in investing tenderness with all the attractiveness of virtue. They ought, rather, to teach the young to distrust the illusions of love, to flee the error of a blind penchant which alway believes that it founds itself on esteem, and to be afraid of confiding a virtuous heart to an object that is sometimes unworthy of its attentions. I know of no other play than the *Misanthrope* in which the hero made a bad choice.* To make the misanthrope fall in love was nothing; the stroke of genius was to make him fall in love with a coquette. All the rest of the theatre is a treasury of perfect women. One would say that they have all taken refuge there. Is this a faithful likeness of society? Is this the way to render suspect a passion which destroys so many well-endowed persons? We are almost made to believe that a decent man is obliged to be in love and that a woman who is loved can be nothing other than virtuous. In this way we are very well instructed indeed!

Once more, I do not undertake to judge if we do well or ill in founding the principal interest of the theatre on love. But I do say that, if its pictures are sometimes dangerous, they are always so, whatever may be done to disguise them. I say that it is to speak in bad faith or in ignorance when its impressions are expected to

* Add *Le Marchand de Londres*,[49] an admirable play the moral of which is more to the point than that of any French play I know.

be rectified by other foreign impressions which do not accompany them to the heart, or which the heart has soon separated out—impressions which even disguise the dangers and give to this perfidious sentiment a new charm with which it destroys those who abandon themselves to it.

Whether we deduce from the nature of the theatre in general its best possible forms, or whether we examine all that the learning of an enlightened age and people has done for the perfection of ours, I believe that we can conclude from these diverse considerations that the moral effect of the theatre can never be good or salutary in itself, since, in reckoning only its advantages, we find no kind of real utility without drawbacks which outweigh it. Now, as a consequence of its very lack of utility, the theatre, which can do nothing to improve morals [manners], can do much toward changing them. In encouraging all our penchants, it gives a new ascendency to those which dominate us. The continual emotion which is felt in the theatre excites us, enervates us, enfeebles us, and makes us less able to resist our passions. And the sterile interest taken in virtue serves only to satisfy our vanity without obliging us to practice it. Hence, those of my compatriots who do not disapprove of the theatre in itself are in error.

VI

BEYOND these effects of the theatre, which are relative to what is performed, there are others no less necessary which relate directly to the stage and to the persons who perform; and it is to them that the previously mentioned Genevans attribute the taste for luxury, adornment, and dissipation, whose introduction among us they rightly fear. It is not only the frequenting of actors, but also the frequenting of the theatre, which, because of the costumes and jewelry of the players, can introduce this taste. If the theatre had no other effect than to interrupt the course of civil and domestic affairs at certain hours and to offer an assured resource to idleness, it is impossible that the opportunity of going every day to the same place to forget oneself and becoming involved with foreign objects should not give other habits to the citizen and form new morals [manners] for him. But will these changes be advantageous or harmful? This is a question that depends less on the consideration of the theatre than on that of the spectators. It is certain that these changes will bring them all pretty nearly to the same point. It is, then, from the situation of each at the beginning that the differences must be estimated.

When amusements are by their nature indifferent (and I am willing to consider the theatre as such for now), it is the nature of the occupations which they interrupt that causes them to be judged good or bad, especially when the amusements are engaging enough to become occupations themselves and to substitute the taste for them in place of that for work. Reason dictates the encouragement of the amusements of people whose occupations are harmful, and the turning-away from the same amusements of those whose occupations are beneficial. Another general consideration is that it is not good to leave the choice of their amusements to idle and corrupted men lest they think up ones which conform to their vicious inclinations and become as mischievous in their pleasures as in their business. But let a simple and hard-working people relax from its labors when and as it pleases; one need never fear that it will abuse this liberty, and one need not trouble oneself looking for agreeable recreations for it. For, just as little preparation is needed for the food that is seasoned by abstinence and hunger, not much is needed for the pleasures of men exhausted by fatigue, for whom repose alone is a very sweet pleasure. In a big city, full of scheming, idle people without religion or principle, whose imagination, depraved by sloth, inactivity, the love of pleasure, and great needs, engenders only monsters and inspires only crimes; in a big city, where morals [manners] and honor are nothing because each, easily hiding his conduct from the public eye, shows himself only by his reputation and is esteemed only for his riches; in a big city, I say, the police can never increase the number of pleasures permitted too much or apply itself too much to making them agreeable in order to deprive individuals of the temptation of seeking more dangerous ones. Since preventing them from occupying themselves is to prevent them from doing harm, two hours a day stolen from the activity of vice prevents the twelfth part of the crimes that would be committed. And all the discussions in cafés and other refuges of the do-nothings and rascals of the place occasioned by plays seen or to be seen are also that much the more gained by family men, either for their daughters' honor or that of their wives, or for their purse or that of their sons.

But in small cities, in less populated places where individuals, always in the public eye, are born censors of one another and where the police can easily watch everyone, contrary maxims must be followed. If there are industry, arts, and manufactures, care must be taken against offering distractions which relax the greedy interest that finds its pleasures in its efforts and enriches the prince from the avarice of his subjects. If the country, without commerce, nourishes its inhabitants in inaction, far from fomenting idleness in them, to which they are already only too susceptible because of their simple and easy life, their life must be rendered insufferable in constraining them, by dint of boredom, to employ time usefully which they could not abuse. I see that in Paris, where everything is judged by appearances because there is no leisure to examine anything, it is believed, on the basis of the apparent inactivity and listlessness which strikes one at first glance in provincial towns, that the inhabitants, plunged in a stupid inactivity, either simply vegetate or only pester one another and quarrel. This is an error which could easily be corrected if it were remembered that most of the literary men who shine in Paris and most of the useful discoveries and new inventions come from these despised provinces. Stay some time in a little town where you had at first believed you would find only automatons; not only will you soon see there men a great deal more sensible than your big-city monkeys, but you will rarely fail to discover in obscurity there some ingenious man who will surprise you by his talents and his works, who you will surprise even more in admiring them, and who, in showing you prodigies of work, patience, and industry, will think he is showing you only what is ordinary at Paris. Such is the simplicity of true genius. It is neither scheming nor busybodyish; it knows not the path of honors and fortune nor dreams of seeking it; it compares itself to no one; all its resources are within itself; indifferent to insult and hardly conscious of praise, if it is aware of itself, it does not assign itself a place and enjoys itself without appraising itself.

In a little town, proportionately less activity is unquestionably to be found than in a capital, because the passions are less intense and the needs less pressing, but more original spirits, more inventive industry, more really new things are found there because the people are less imitative; having few models, each draws more from himself and puts more of his own in everything he does; because the human mind, less spread out, less drowned in vulgar opinions, elaborates itself and ferments better in tranquil solitude; because, in seeing less, more is imagined; finally, because less pressed for time, there is more leisure to extend and digest one's ideas.

I remember having seen in my youth a very pleasant sight, one perhaps unique on earth, in the vicinity of Neufchatel; an entire mountain covered with dwellings each one of which constitutes the center of the lands which belong to it, so that these houses, separated by distances as equal as the fortunes of the proprietors, offer to the numerous inhabitants of this mountain both the tranquillity of a retreat and the sweetness of society. These happy farmers, all in comfortable circumstances, free of poll-taxes, duties, commissioners, and forced labor, cultivate with all possible care lands the produce of which is theirs, and employ the leisure that tillage leaves them to make countless artifacts with their hands and to put to use the inventive genius which nature gave them. In the winter especially, a time when the deep snows prevent easy communication, each, warmly closed up with his big family in his pretty and clean wooden house,* which he has himself built, busies himself with enjoyable labors which drive boredom from his sanctuary and add to his well-being. Never did carpenter, locksmith, glazier, or turner enter this country; each is everything for himself, no one is anything for another. Among the many comfortable and even elegant pieces of furniture which make up their household and adorn their lodgings, none is ever seen which was not made by the hand of the master. They still have leisure time left over in which to invent and make all sorts of instruments of steel, wood, and cardboard which they sell to foreigners; many of these even get to Paris, among others those little wooden clocks that have been seen there during the last few years. They also make some of iron, and even make watches. And, what seems unbelievable, each joins in himself all the various crafts into which watchmaking is subdivided and makes all his tools himself.

This is not all. They have useful books and are tolerably well educated. They reason sensibly about everything and about many things with brilliance.** They make syphons, magnets, spectacles, pumps, barometers, and cameras obscura. Their tapestry consists of masses of instruments of every sort; you would take a farmer's living room for a mechanic's workshop and for a laboratory in experimental physics. All know how to sketch, paint, and calculate a bit; most play the flute, many know something of the principles of

* I can hear a Paris wit, provided he is not himself giving the reading, protesting at this point, as at many others, and learnedly proving to the ladies (for it is chiefly to ladies that these gentlemen make proofs) that it is impossible that a wooden house be warm. Vulgar falsehood! Error in physics! Alas, poor author! As for me, I think the demonstration is irrefutable. All that I know is that the Swiss spend their winter warmly in the midst of snows in wooden houses.

** I can cite, as an example, a man of merit well known in Paris and more than once honored by the suffrages of the Academy of Sciences. It is M. Rivaz, an illustrious Valaisan. I know that he does not have many equals among his countrymen; but it was in living as they do that he learned how to surpass them.

music and can sing true. These arts are not taught them by masters but are passed down, as it were, by tradition. Of those I saw who knew music, one would tell me he had learned it from his father, another from his aunt, and a third from his cousin; some thought they had always known it. One of their most frequent amusements is to sing psalms in four parts with their wives and children; and one is amazed to hear issuing from rustic cabins the strong and masculine harmony of Goudimel so long forgotten by our learned artists.

I could no more tire of wandering among these charming dwellings than could the inhabitants of offering me the frankest hospitality. Unhappily I was young; my curiosity was only that of a child, and I thought more of amusing myself than learning. In thirty years the few observations I made have been erased from my memory. I only remember that I continually admired in these singular men an amazing combination of delicacy and simplicity that would be believed to be almost incompatible and that I have never since observed elsewhere. Otherwise I remember nothing of their morals [manners], their society, or characters. Today, when I would bring other eyes to it, am I never again to see that happy land? Alas, it is on the road to my own.

After this sketch, let us suppose that at the summit of the mountain of which I have spoken, amidst the dwellings, a standing and inexpensive theatre be established under the pretext, for example, of providing a decent recreation for people otherwise constantly busy and able to bear this little expense. Let us further suppose that they get a taste for this theatre, and let us investigate what will be the results of its establishment.

I see, in the first place, that their labors will cease to be their amusements and that, as soon as they have a new amusement, it will undermine their taste for the old ones; zeal will no longer furnish so much leisure nor the same inventions. Moreover, everyday there will be real time lost for those who go to the theatre, and they will no longer go right back to work, since their thoughts will be full of what they have just seen; they will talk about it and think about it. Consequently, slackening of work: first disadvantage.

However little is paid at the door, they do pay. It is still an expense that was not previously made. It costs for oneself and for one's wife and children when they are taken along, and sometimes they must be. In addition, a worker does not present himself in an assembly in his working clothes. He must put on his Sunday clothes, change linen, and powder and shave himself more often; all this costs time and money. Increase of expenses: second disadvantage.

Less assiduous work and larger expenses exact a compensation; it will be found in the price of what is produced, which must be made dearer. Many merchants, driven off by this increase, will leave the Mountaineers* and supply themselves from the neighboring Swiss who, being no less industrious, will have no theatre and will not increase their prices. Decrease in trade: third disadvantage.

During bad weather the roads are not passable; and, since the company must live in these seasons too, it will not interrupt its performances. Hence, making the theatre accessible at all seasons cannot be avoided. In the winter, roads must be made in the snow and, perhaps, paved; and God grant that they do not put up lanterns. Now there are public expenses and, in consequence, contributions from individuals. Establishment of taxes: fourth disadvantage.

The wives of the Mountaineers, going first to see and then to be seen, will want to be dressed and dressed with distinction. The wife of the chief magistrate will not want to present herself at the theatre attired like the schoolmaster's. The schoolmaster's wife will strive to be attired like the chief magistrate's. Out of this will soon emerge a competition in dress which will ruin the husbands, will perhaps win them over, and which will find countless new ways to get around the sumptuary laws. Introduction of luxury: fifth disadvantage.

All the rest is easy to imagine. Without taking into consideration the other disadvantages of which I have spoken or will speak

* This is the name given to the inhabitants of this mountain in that country.

in what follows, without investigating the sort of theatre and its moral effects, I confine myself to arguments which have to do with work and gain; and I believe I have shown, by an evident inference, how a prosperous people, but one which owes its well-being to its industry, exchanging reality for appearance, ruins itself at the very moment it wants to shine.

Moreover, my supposition ought not to be objected to as chimerical. I present it merely as such and only want to render its inevitable consequences more or less obvious. Take away some circumstances and you will find other Mountaineers elsewhere; and *mutatis mutandis*, the example has its application.

Thus, even if it were true that the theatre is not bad in itself, it would remain to be investigated if it does not become so in respect to the people for which it is destined. In certain places it will be useful for attracting foreigners; for increasing the circulation of money; for stimulating artists; for varying the fashions; for occupying those who are too rich or aspire to be so; for making them less mischievous; for distracting the people from its miseries; for making it forget its leaders in seeing its buffoons; for maintaining and perfecting taste when decency is lost; for covering the ugliness of vice with the polish of forms; in a word, for preventing bad morals [manners] from degenerating into brigandage. In other places it would only serve to destroy the love of work; to discourage industry; to ruin individuals; to inspire them with the taste for idleness; to make them seek for the means of subsistence without doing anything; to render a people inactive and slack; to prevent it from seeing the public and private goals with which it ought to busy itself; to turn prudence to ridicule; to substitute a theatrical jargon for the practice of the virtues; to make metaphysic of all morality; to turn citizens into wits, housewives into bluestockings, and daughters into sweethearts out of the drama. The general effect will be the same on all men; but the men thus changed will suit their country more or less. In becoming equals, the bad will gain and the good will lose still more; all will contract a soft disposition and a spirit of inaction which will deprive the good of great virtues but will keep the bad from meditating great crimes.

From these new reflections results a consequence directly opposed to the one I drew from the first,[50] namely, that when the people is corrupted, the theatre is good for it, and bad for it when it is itself good. It would, hence, seem that these two contrary effects would destroy one another and the theatre remain indifferent to both. But there is this difference: the effect which reenforces the good and the bad, since it is drawn from the spirit of the plays, is subject, as are they, to countless modifications which reduce it to practically nothing, while the effect which changes the good into bad and the bad into good, resulting from the very existence of a theatre, is a real, constant one which returns every day and must finally prevail.

It follows from this that, in order to decide if it is proper or not to establish a theatre in a certain town, we must know in the first place if the morals [manners] are good or bad there, a question concerning which it is perhaps not for me to answer with regard to us. However that may be, all that I can admit about this is that it is true that the drama will not harm us if nothing at all can harm us any more.

VII

To forestall the disadvantages which could be born of the actors' example, you would want them to be forced to be decent men. By this means, you say, we would have both theatre and morals [manners], and we would join the advantages of both. Theatre and morals! This would really be something to see,[51] so much the more so as it would be the first time. But what are the means that you indicate to us for restraining the actors? Severe and well-executed laws. This is to admit at least that the actors must be restrained and that the means of doing it are not easy. Severe laws? The first is not to tolerate them. If we infringe this one, what will become of the severity of the others? Well-executed laws? The question is whether this is possible; for the force of the laws has its measure, and the force of the vices that they repress has one too. It is only after one has compared these two quantities and found that the former surpasses the latter that the execution of the laws can be depended upon. The knowledge of these relations constitutes the true legislator's science. For if it had to do only with publishing edict after edict, regulation after regulation, to remedy abuses as they arise, doubtless many very fine things would be said, but which, for the most part, would remain without effect and would serve as indications of what would need to be done rather than as means toward executing it. On the whole, the institution of laws is not such a marvelous thing that any man of sense and equity could not easily find those which, well observed, would be the most beneficial for society. Where is the least student of the law who cannot erect a moral code as pure as that of Plato's laws? But this is not the only issue. The problem is to adapt this code to the people for which it is made and to the things about which it decrees to such an extent that its execution follows from the very conjunction of these relations; it is to impose on the people, after the fashion of Solon, less the best laws in themselves than the best of which it admits in the given situation. Otherwise, it is better to let the disorders subsist than to forestall them, or take steps thereto, by laws which will not be observed. For without remedying the evil, this degrades the laws too.

Another observation, no less important, is that matters of morals [manners] and universal justice are not arranged, as are those of private justice and strict right, by edicts and laws; or, if sometimes the laws influence morals [manners], it is when the laws draw their force from them. Then they return to morals [manners] this same force by a sort of reaction well known to real statesmen. The first function of the Spartan ephors upon taking office was a public proclamation in which they enjoined the citizens not to observe but to love the laws, so that their observation would not be hard.[52] This proclamation, which was not an idle formula, shows perfectly the spirit of the Spartan regime in which laws and morals [manners], intimately united in the hearts of the citizens, made, as it were, only one single body. But let us not flatter ourselves that we shall see Sparta reborn in the lap of commerce and the love of gain. If we had the same maxims, a theatre could be established at Geneva without any risk; for never would citizen or townsman set foot in it.

By what means can the government get a hold on morals [manners]? I answer that it is by public opinion. If our habits in retirement are born of our own sentiments, in society they are born of others' opinions. When we do not live in ourselves but in others, it is their judgments which guide everything. Nothing appears good or desirable to individuals which the public has not judged to be such, and the only happiness which most men know is to be esteemed happy.

As to the choice of instruments proper to the direction of public opinion, that is another question which it would be superfluous to resolve for you and which it is not here the place to resolve for the multitude. I shall content myself with showing by an evident example that these instruments are neither laws nor punishments nor any sort of coercive means. This example is before your eyes; I take it from your country; it is the tribunal of the marshals of France established as supreme judges on points of honor.[53]

What was the reason for this institution? It was established to change public opinion about duels, the redress of offenses and the occasions when a brave man is obliged, under penalty of disgrace, to get satisfaction for an affront with sword in hand. From this it follows:

First, that, force having no power over minds, it was necessary to dismiss with the greatest of care every vestige of violence from the tribunal established to work this change. The very word *tribunal* was badly conceived; I should prefer *Court of Honor*. Its sole arms ought to have been honor and disgrace—never useful recompense, never corporal punishment, no prison, no arrests, no armed guards, simply an apparitor who would have served his summonses by touching the defendant with a white rod, without any other constraint following upon that to make him appear. It is true that not to appear before the judges on the specified date would be to confess to being without defense and to condemn oneself. The natural consequence would be a mark of disgrace, degradation in nobility, unfitness to serve the king in his tribunals and armies, and other punishments of this sort which have directly to do with opinion or are a necessary effect of it.

In the second place, it follows that, to uproot the public prejudice, judges of great authority on the matter in question were needed. And, on this point, the founder entered perfectly into the spirit of the institution. For, in a very warlike nation, who can better judge of the just occasions to show one's courage and on which offended honor demands satisfaction, than old soldiers laden with honorable titles who have grown gray with their laurels, and proved a hundred times at the cost of their blood that they are not unaware when duty demands that it be spilled.

It follows, in the third place, that, since nothing is more independent of the supreme power than the judgment of the public, the sovereign ought to have taken care in all things not to mix his arbitrary decisions in with the decrees meant to represent and, what is more, to determine this judgment. He ought, on the contrary, to have endeavoured to put the Court of Honor above himself as though he were subject to its respectable sentences himself. It was hence wrong to begin by condemning all duelists indiscriminately to death; this created straight-off a shocking opposition between honor and the law; for even the law cannot oblige anyone to dishonor himself. If the whole people has judged that a man is a poltroon, the king, in spite of all his power, can declare him brave all he wishes and no one will believe a bit of it; and the man, passing then for a poltroon who wants to be honored by force, will be only the more despised. As to what the edicts say, that to fight is to offend God, this is undoubtedly a very pious opinion; but the civil law is no judge of sins, and every time that the sovereign authority wants to interpose itself in the conflicts between honor and religion, it will be compromised on both sides. The same edicts reason no better when they say that instead of fighting, the marshals must be consulted; to condemn combat without distinction or reserve in this way is to begin by judging beforehand what is referred to their judgment. It is known that it is not permitted to them to accord a duel even when insulted honor has no other recourse; and, according to the prejudices of society, there are many such cases. For, as to the ceremonious satisfactions which have been offered to the offended persons, they are really child's play.

By artfully manipulating the maxim that a man has the right to accept a compensation and pardon his enemy, it can be gradually substituted for the ferocious prejudice it attacks; but it is not the same when the honor of persons is attacked with whom our own is connected. From this moment on there is no further accomodation possible. If my father has been slapped, my sister, wife, or mistress insulted, shall I preserve my honor in selling their's cheaply? There are neither marshals nor satisfactions which suffice; I must get revenge for them or dishonor myself; the edicts leave me only the choice of torture or disgrace. To cite an example which relates to my subject, is it not a well-balanced harmony between the spirit of the stage and that of the laws, when we go to the theatre to applaud the same Cid whom we would go to see hanged at the Grève?[54]

Thus we can do what we like; neither reason, nor virtue, nor laws will vanquish public opinion, so long as the art of changing it has not been found. Once again, this art has nothing to do with violence. If they were put into practice, the established means would serve only to punish the brave and spare the cowards; but, happily, they are too absurd to be used and have served only to change the name of duels. How ought it to have been gone about? Private combats, it seems to me, ought to have been submitted absolutely to the jurisdiction of the marshals, either to judge them, to prevent them, or even to permit them. Not only ought they to have been allowed the right to grant combat when they judged it appropriate; but it was important that they sometimes exercise this right, if only to rid the public of an idea rather difficult to do away with and which by itself annuls all their authority, which is, that in the affairs which pass before them, they follow less their own sentiment than the will of the prince. Then there would have been no shame in asking them to permit combat on a necessary occasion; there would have been none even in refraining from doing so when the reasons for granting it were not judged sufficient. But there always will be shame to say to them: I have been offended; arrange it so that I will not have to fight.

By this means, all secret challenges would surely have fallen into disrepute, since, honor offended being able to defend itself, and courage being able to show itself on the field of honor, those who had hidden themselves to fight would have been quite justly suspect, and those whom the Court of Honor judged to have fought badly* would have been turned over to the criminal courts as vile assassins. I admit that, since many duels would have been judged only after the fact and others even solemnly authorized, it would have, at first, cost the lives of some brave men; but it would have been to save the lives of countless others afterwards; whereas, from the blood which is spilled in spite of the edicts, there arises a reason for spilling even more.

What would have happened afterwards? As the Court of Honor acquired authority over the opinion of the people by the wisdom and the weight of its decisions, it would little by little have become more severe until the legitimate occasions had been reduced to

---

* Badly, that is to say not only in a cowardly and fraudulent way, but unjustly, and without sufficient reason, which would naturally be presumed of any affair not brought before the tribunal.

nothingness, the point of honor had changed principles, and duels were entirely abolished. In truth, all this effort did not have to be taken, but also a useless institution was founded. If duels are rarer today, it is not because they are despised or punished, but because the morals [manners] have changed.* And the proof that this change comes from entirely different causes in which the government has no part, the proof that public opinion has in no wise changed on this point, is that, after so many ill-conceived pains, any gentleman who does not get satisfaction for an affront with sword in hand is no less dishonored than before.

A fourth consequence of the object of the same institution is that, no man being able to live civilly without honor, all the estates in which one carries a sword, from prince to private soldier, and even all the estates in which one is not worn, ought to be under the jurisdiction of this Court of Honor; the former to give an account of their conduct and their actions, the others of their speeches and their maxims; all equally subject to being honored or stigmatized according to the conformity or the opposition of their lives or sentiments to the principles of honor established in the nation and gradually reformed by the tribunal on the basis of those of justice and reason. To limit this competence to the nobles and the soldiers is to cut the shoots and leave the root; for if the point of honor makes the nobility act, it makes the people talk; the former fight only because the others judge them; and to change the actions of which public esteem is the object, the judgments that are made about them must be changed beforehand. I am convinced that we

* Formerly, men quarrelled in taverns; they have been given a distaste for this crude pleasure by being given others at a low price. Formerly, they slew one another for a mistress; in living more familiarly with women, they have found that it was not worth the effort to fight for them. Drunkenness and love set aside, there remain few important subjects for dispute. In society one now fights only over gambling. Soldiers fight only over undue favor or in order not to be forced to leave the service. In this age of enlightenment, everyone knows how to calculate to the penny the worth of his honor and his life.

will never succeed in working these changes without bringing about the intervention of women, on whom men's way of thinking in large measure depends.

From this principle it follows, moreover, that the tribunal ought to be more or less dreaded in the various ranks in proportion to their having more or less honor to lose according to the vulgar ideas which must always be taken here as rules. If the institution is well constructed, the grandees and the princes ought to tremble at the very name of *Court of Honor*. When it was established, all the personal quarrels then existing among the first men of the realm ought to have been brought before it; the tribunal would have judged them definitively in so far as is possible by the laws of honor alone; these judgments would have been severe; there would have been surrender of privilege and rank, personal and independent of the right of position, prohibition to bear arms or to appear before the prince, or other similar punishments, nothing in themselves, grievous in opinion, up to total disgrace which would have been regarded as the capital punishment handed down by the Court of Honor. All these punishments would have had, with the support of the supreme authority, the same effects that public judgment naturally has when force does not annul its decisions; the tribunal would not have pronounced about trifles but would have never done anything halfway; the king himself would have been summoned when he threw his cane out the window for fear, he said, of striking a gentleman;* he would have appeared, as the defendant, with his opponent; he would have been solemnly judged and condemned to make amends for the indirect affront done the gentleman; and the tribunal would have at the same time awarded him a prize for the monarch's moderation in anger. This prize, which ought to have been a very simple but conspicuous mark, worn by the king throughout his life, would have been, it seems to me, an ornament

* M. de Lauzun. This, in my view, would have been a well-administered caning.[55]

more honorable than those of royalty, and I do not doubt that it would have become the subject of the refrains of more than one poet. It is certain that, as to honor, the kings themselves are more subject than anyone to public judgment and can, consequently, without lowering themselves, appear before the tribunal which represents it. Louis XIV was capable of doing such things; and I believe he would have done them if someone had suggested them to him.

With all of these precautions and other similar ones, it is very doubtful if success could have been attained, because such an institution is entirely contrary to the spirit of monarchy. But it is quite certain that for having neglected them, for having wanted to mix force and laws in matters of prejudice and change the point of honor by violence, the royal authority has been compromised and laws which went beyond their power have been rendered contemptible.

However, in what did this prejudice consist that was to be done away with? In the wildest and most barbarous opinion which ever entered the human mind, namely, that bravery can take the place of all the duties of society; that a man is no longer a cheat, rascal, or slanderer, that he is civil, humane, and polite when he knows how to fight; that falsehood is changed into truth, robbery becomes legitimate, perfidy honesty, infidelity praiseworthy, as soon as all this is maintained sword in hand; that an affront is always made good by a sword thrust; that a man is never wrong in relation to another provided that he kill him. There is, I admit, another kind of affair in which politeness is mixed with cruelty and men are killed only by accident, that in which one fights to the first blood. To the first blood! Great God! And what do you want to do with this blood, ferocious beast? Do you want to drink it? How can these things be thought of without emotion? Such are the prejudices that the kings of France, armed with the whole public force, have attacked in vain. Opinion, queen of the world, is not subject to the power of kings; they are themselves her first slaves.

I bring to an end this long digression which unhappily will not be the last; and, from this perhaps too dazzling example, *si parva licet componere magnis*,[56] I return to simpler applications. One of the inevitable effects of a theatre established in a town as little as ours will be to change our maxims, or, if you please, our prejudices and our public opinions, which will necessarily change our morals [manners] for others, better or worse I do not yet say, but assuredly less appropriate to our constitution. I ask, Sir, by what efficient law will you remedy that? If the government can do much in morals [manners], it is only in its primitive institution; when once it has determined them, not only does it no longer have the power to change them without itself changing, it has great difficulty in maintaining them against the inevitable accidents which attack them and the natural inclination which corrupts them. Public opinions, although so difficult to govern, are nevertheless in themselves very mobile and changing. Chance, countless accidental causes, countless unforeseen circumstances, do what force and reason could not; or, rather, it is precisely because chance directs them that force can do nothing; like the dice which leave the hand, whatever impulsion is given them does not bring up the desired point any more easily.

All that human wisdom can do is to forestall changes, to arrest from afar all that brings them on. But, once they are tolerated and authorized, we are rarely master of their effects and cannot be held answerable for them. How then shall we prevent those of which we have voluntarily introduced the cause? In imitation of the institution of which I have just spoken, will you propose to institute censors? We already have them;* and if the whole force of this tribunal barely suffices to maintain us as we are, when we have added a new inclination to the penchant of morals [manners], what will it do to arrest this progress? It is clear that it will no

* The Consistory and the Chamber of the Reformation.[57]

longer suffice. The first sign of its impotence to forestall the abuses of the drama will be to permit its establishment. For it is easy to foresee that these two institutions will not long exist side by side, and that the drama will turn the censors to ridicule or the censors will drive out the actors.

VIII

BUT it is not only the insufficiency of the laws in repressing bad morals [manners] when their cause is allowed to subsist that is the question here. It will be found, I foresee, that, my mind being filled with the abuses that the theatre necessarily engenders and with the general impossibility of preventing these abuses, I do not respond precisely enough to the expedient proposed, which is, to have actors who are decent men and women, that is to say, to make them such. At bottom, this special discussion is not really very necessary, since all that I have said up to now about the effects of the drama is independent of the morals [manners] of the actors, and would take place even if they profited from the lessons which you urge us to give them and became, under our guidance, so many models of virtue. However, out of consideration for the sentiment of those of my compatriots who see no other danger in the drama than the bad example of the actors, I want to investigate whether, even on the basis of their supposition, this expedient is practicable with some hope of success and whether it ought to suffice to reassure them.

To begin by observing the facts before reasoning about the causes, I see in general that the estate of the actor is one of license and bad morals [manners]; that the men are given to disorder; that the women lead a scandalous life; that both, avaricious and spendthrift at the same time, always overwhelmed by debts and always spending money in torrents, are as little controlled in their dissipations as they are scrupulous about the means of providing for them. I see, moreover, that in every country their profession is one that dishonors, that those who exercise it, excommunicated or not, are everywhere despised;* and that even in Paris, where they are most respected and behave better than anywhere else, a man of the middle class would be afraid to frequent these same actors who are seen everyday at the tables of the great. A third observation, no less important, is that this disdain is stronger everywhere the morals [manners] are purer, and there are innocent and simple countries where the actor's profession almost horrifies. These are incontestable facts. You will tell me that they are only the results of prejudice. I agree; but since these prejudices are universal, a universal cause must be sought, and I cannot see that it can be found elsewhere than in the profession itself to which they relate. To that you answer that the actors only make themselves contemptible because they are held in contempt. But why should they have been held in contempt if they had not been contemptible? Why would their estate have been worse thought of than others if there were nothing which distinguished it from them? This is perhaps what must be considered before justifying the actors at the expense of the public.

I could impute these prejudices to the declamations of the priests, if I did not find them established among the Romans before the birth of Christianity and not only vaguely current in the spirit of the people but authorized by express laws which declared the actors disreputable, stripped them of the name and rights of Roman citizens, and put the actresses in the class of prostitutes. Here every reason is missing, other than that which is drawn from the nature of the thing. The pagan priests and the devout were more in favor of, than against, the theatrical entertainments which were parts

* If the English buried the celebrated Oldfield[58] at the side of their kings, it was not her profession but her talent that they wanted to honor. With them, great talents ennoble in the smallest stations, little ones abase in the most illustrious. And, as to the actor's profession, the bad and the mediocre are despised in London as much as anywhere else.

of the games consecrated to religion,* and had no interest in disparaging the theatre nor did they do so. Nevertheless, as soon as this was the case, it was possible to criticize, as you do, the inconsistency of dishonoring people whom we protect, pay, and pension. To tell the truth, it does not seem so strange to me as it does to you; for it is sometimes proper for the state to encourage and protect dishonorable but useful professions, without those who exercise them being more highly considered for that.

I read somewhere that this stigma was less attached to real actors than to histrions and jesters who soil their entertainment with indecency and obscenity. But this distinction is indefensible; for the words, *actor* and *histrion*, were perfectly synonymous and had no difference other than that one was Greek and the other Etruscan. Cicero, in his book *On The Orator*,[60] calls the two greatest actors which Rome ever had, Esopus and Roscius, histrions. In his defense of the latter, Cicero pities so decent a man for exercising so indecent a profession.[61] Far from distinguishing between the actors, histrions, and jesters, or between the actors of tragedy and those of comedy, the law indiscriminately covers all those who step on the stage with the same opprobrium. *Quisquis in scenam prodierit ait Praetor, infamis est.*[62] It is true, only, that this opprobrium attached itself less to performing as such than to making a profession of it, inasmuch as the Roman youth publicly performed the *Atellanae* or *Exodia* [63] at the end of the long plays without dishonor. With this exception, it can be observed in countless places that all the actors, without distinction, were slaves and were treated as such when the public was not satisfied with them.

I know of only one people which did not have the same maxims as all the others about this; that is the Greeks. It is certain that among them the profession of the theatre was so little indecent that Greece furnishes examples of actors charged with certain public

---

* Livy says that the theatrical games were introduced into Rome in the year 390 [A.U.C.] on the occasion of a plague which they wanted to stop.[59] Today the theatres would be closed for the same cause, and surely this would be more reasonable.

functions either in the state or on embassies. But the reasons for this exception can easily be found. (1) Since tragedy, as well as comedy, was invented by the Greeks, they could not in advance put a mark of contempt on an estate the effects of which they did not yet know, and, when they began to be known, public opinion was already fixed. (2) Since tragedy had something sacred in its origin, at first its actors were regarded as priests rather than buffoons. (3) Since all the subjects of the plays were drawn exclusively from the national antiquities which the Greeks idolized, they saw in these actors less men who played fables than educated citizens who performed the history of their country so that it could be seen by their fellow citizens. (4) This people, so enthusiastic about its liberty as to believe that the Greeks were the only men free by nature,* recalled with a vivid sentiment of pleasure its ancient misfortunes and the crimes of its masters. These great depictions ceaselessly instructed this people who could not prevent themselves from feeling some respect for the organs of this instruction. (5) Tragedy was at first played only by men, so that in their theatre this scandalous mixture of men and women, which makes of our theatres so many schools of bad morals [manners], was not to be seen. (6) Finally, their performances had none of the meanness of today's; their theatres were not built by interest and avarice; they were not closed up in dark prisons; their actors had no need to make collections from the spectators or to count out of the corner of their eye the number of people whom they saw coming in the door to be sure of their supper.

These great and proud entertainments, given under the sky before a whole nation, presented on all sides only combats, victories, prizes, objects capable of insipiring the Greeks with an ardent emulation and of warming their hearts with sentiments of honor and glory. It is in the midst of this imposing array, so fit to elevate one and stir the soul, that the actors, animated with the same zeal,

---

* Iphigenia says it expressly in the tragedy of Euripides which bears the name of this princess.

shared, according to their talents, the honors rendered to the conquerors of the games, often the first men of the nation. I am not surprised that, far from abasing them, their profession, exercised in this manner, gave them that pride of courage and that noble disinterestedness which seemed sometimes to raise the actor to the level of his role. With all of this, never was Greece, Sparta excepted, cited as an example of good morals [manners]; and Sparta, which tolerated no theatre,* was not concerned with honoring those who appeared in it.

Let us return to the Romans who, far from following the example of the Greeks in this respect, set an entirely contrary one. If their laws declared the actors disreputable, was it with the design of dishonoring the profession? What would have been the benefit of so cruel a provision? They did not dishonor it, they only gave authoritative expression to the dishonor which is inseparable from it. For never do good laws change the nature of things; they only follow it, and only such laws are obeyed. The point is not to begin by crying out against prejudices but first to know if they are only prejudices, whether the actor's profession is really not dishonorable in itself. For if unfortunately it is, for all that we decree that it is not, rather than rehabilitating it, we will only abase ourselves.

What is the talent of the actor? It is the art of counterfeiting himself, of putting on another character than his own, of appearing different than he is, of becoming passionate in cold blood, of saying what he does not think as naturally as if he really did think it, and, finally, of forgetting his own place by dint of taking another's. What is the profession of the actor? It is a trade in which he performs for money, submits himself to the disgrace and the affronts that others buy the right to give him, and puts his person publicly on sale. I beg every sincere man to tell if he does not feel in the depths of his soul that there is something servile and base in this traffic of oneself. You philosophers, who have the pretention of being so far above prejudices, would you not all die of shame if,

* Concerning this error, see the letter of M. Leroy.[64]

ignominiously gotten up as kings, you had to take on in the eyes of the public a different role than your own and expose your majesties to the jeers of the populace? What, then, is the spirit that the actor receives from his estate? A mixture of abjectness, duplicity, ridiculous conceit, and disgraceful abasement which renders him fit for all sorts of roles except for the most noble of all, that of man, which he abandons.

I know that the actor's playing is not that of a scoundrel who wants to cheat, that he does not intend to be really taken for the person he represents or to be believed affected by the passions he imitates, and that, in presenting this imitation for what it is, he renders it entirely innocent. And I do not precisely accuse him of being a deceiver but of cultivating by profession the talent of deceiving men and of becoming adept in habits which can be innocent only in the theatre and can serve everywhere else only for doing harm. Will these men, so well adorned, so well practiced in the tone of gallantry and in the accents of passion, never abuse this art to seduce young persons? Will these thieving valets, so subtle with tongue and hand on the stage, never make a useful application of their art in the interests of a profession more expensive than lucrative, will they never have any useful distractions? Will they never take the purse of a prodigal son or of an avaricious father for that of Léander or Argan?* In all things the temptation to do evil increases with its facility; and actors must be more virtuous than other men if they are not more corrupt.

The orator and the preacher, it could be said, make use of their persons as does the actor. The difference is, however, very great. When the orator appears in public, it is to speak and not to show himself off; he represents only himself; he fills only his own role,

---

* This has been objected to as extravagant and ridiculous, and rightly so. There is no vice of which actors are less accused than thievery. Their profession, which keeps them very busy and even gives them sentiments of honor in certain respects, removes them from such baseness. I leave this passage because I have made it a law for myself to remove nothing; but I disavow it in full public view as a very great injustice.[65]

speaks only in his own name, says, or ought to say, only what he thinks; the man and the role being the same, he is in his place; he is in the situation of any citizen who fulfils the functions of his estate. But an actor on the stage, displaying other sentiments than his own, saying only what he is made to say, often representing a chimerical being, annihilates himself, as it were, and is lost in his hero. And, in this forgetting of the man, if something remains of him, it is used as the plaything of the spectators. What shall I say of those who seem to be afraid of having too much merit as they are and who degrade themselves to the point of playing characters whom they would be quite distressed to resemble? It is certainly a very bad thing to see so many rascals playing the roles of decent men in society; but is there anything more odious, more shocking, more ignoble, than a decent man playing a rascal's role in the theatre and using all his talent to make criminal maxims convincing, maxims for which he himself has only disgust?

If all of this only seems to give evidence of a not very respectable profession, the dissoluteness of the actresses should be seen as another source of bad morals [manners] which compels and carries in its wake dissoluteness in the actors. But why is this dissoluteness inevitable? Oh, why! In any other time there would be no need to ask; but, in this age when prejudices reign so proudly and error gives itself the name of philosophy, men, besotted with their vain learning, have closed their minds to the voice of reason and their hearts to that of nature.

In every station, every country, every class, the two sexes have so strong and so natural a relation to one another that the morals [manners] of the one always determine those of the other. Not that these morals [manners] are always the same, but they always have the same degree of goodness, modified by the penchants peculiar to each sex. The English women are gentle and timid. The English men are hard and haughty. From whence does this apparent opposition stem? From the fact that the character of each sex is thus heightened and that it is also the national character to carry everything to the extreme. Apart from this, everything is similar. The two sexes like to live apart; both esteem the pleasures of the table; both gather to drink after the meal, the men wine, the women tea; both indulge in games without them being a rage and make a craft of it rather than a passion; both have a great respect for decent things; both love their country and its laws; both honor conjugal fidelity, and, if they violate it, do not make it an honor to do so; domestic tranquillity pleases both; both are quiet and taciturn; they are both difficult to move; both violent in their passions; for both, love is terrible and tragic, it decides the fate of their days; nothing less is at stake, says Muralt,[66] than losing reason or life in it. Finally, both enjoy themselves in the country, and English ladies like to wander in their solitary parks as much as to go to show themselves off at Vauxhall. From this common taste for solitude arises a taste for the contemplative readings and the novels with which England is inundated.* Thus both, withdrawn more into themselves, give themselves less to frivolous imitations, get more of a taste for the true pleasures of life, and think less of appearing happy than of being so.

I have made especial mention of the English because they are, of all the nations of the world, the one in which the morals [manners] of the two sexes appear at first glance to be most contrary. From their relation in this country we can draw a conclusion about the others. The whole difference consists in the fact that the life of women is a continual development of their morals [manners], whereas, since those of men disappear in the uniformity of business, one must wait to see them in their pleasures to judge of them. Do you want to know men? Study women. This maxim is general, and up to this point everybody will agree with me. But if I add that there are no good morals [manners] for women outside of a withdrawn and domestic life; if I say that the peaceful care of the family and the home are their lot, that the dignity of their sex

---

* They are, like the men, sublime or detestable. In no language whatsoever has a novel the equal of *Clarissa*,[67] or even approaching it, ever been written.

consists in modesty, that shame and chasteness[68] are inseparable from decency for them, that when they seek for men's looks they are already letting themselves be corrupted by them, and that any woman who shows herself off disgraces herself; I will be immediately attacked by this philosophy of a day which is born and dies in the corner of a big city and wishes to smother the cry of nature and the unanimous voice of humankind.

"Popular prejudices!" exclaim some. "Petty errors of childhood. Deceit of the laws and of education! Chasteness is nothing. It is only an invention of the social laws to protect the rights of fathers and husbands and to preserve some order in families. Why should we blush at the needs which nature has given us? Why should we find a motive for shame in an act so indifferent in itself and so beneficial in its effects as the one which leads to the perpetuation of the species? Since the desires are equal on both sides, why should their manifestations be different? Why should one of the sexes deny itself more than the other in the penchants which are common to them both? Why should man have different laws on this point than the animals?"

> *Your whys, says the God, would never end.*[69]

But it is not to man but to his Author that they should be addressed. Is it not absurd that I should have to say why I am ashamed of a natural sentiment, if this shame is no less natural to me than the sentiment itself? I might as well ask myself why I have the sentiment. Is it for me to justify what nature has done? From this line of reasoning, those who do not see why man exists ought to deny that he exists.

I am afraid that these great scrutinizers of God's counsels have weighed His reasons a little lightly. I, who do not pretend to know these reasons, believe that I see some which have escaped them. Whatever they may say about it, the shame which veils the pleasures of love from the eyes of others is something. It is the safeguard that nature has given in common to the two sexes for a time when they are in a state of weakness and forgetfulness of themselves which puts them at the mercy of the first comer; it is thus that it covers their sleep with the shadows of night, so that, during this time of darkness, they will be less exposed to one another's attacks. It is thus that it causes every sick animal to seek isolation and deserted places, so that it can suffer and die in peace, safe from the blows it can no longer fend off.

In relation to the chasteness of women in particular, what gentler arm could this same nature have given to the one it destined to resist? The desires are equal. What does that mean? Are there on both sides the same faculties for their satisfaction? What would become of the human species if the order of attack and defense were changed? The assailant would choose by chance times when victory would be impossible; the assailed would be left in peace when he needs to be vanquished, and pursued without interruption when he is too weak to succumb; in a word, since the power and the will, always in disaccord, would never permit the desires to be mutually shared, love would no longer be the support of nature but its destroyer and plague.

If the two sexes had equally made and received the advances, vain importunity would have never been preserved; the passions, ever languishing in a boring freedom, would have never been excited; the sweetest of all the sentiments would hardly have touched the human heart, and its object would have been badly fulfilled. The apparent obstacle, which seems to keep this object at a distance, is in reality what brings it nearer. The desires, veiled by shame, become only the more seductive; in hindering them, chasteness inflames them. Its fears, its tricks, its reserves, its timid avowals, its tender and naive delicacy, say better what chasteness thinks to hide than passion could have said it without chasteness. It is chasteness which lends value to favors granted and sweetness to rejection. True love possesses really what chasteness alone contests with it; that mixture of weakness and modesty renders it more touching and tenderer; the less it obtains, the more the value of what it does obtain increases, and it is thus that it enjoys both its privations and its pleasures.

"Why," they ask, "should what is not shameful for a man be so for a woman? Why should one of the sexes make a crime for itself out of what the other believes itself permitted?" As if the consequences were the same on both sides! As if all the austère duties of the woman were not derived from the single fact that a child ought to have a father. Even if these important considerations were lacking to me, we would nevertheless still have the same response and it would still be without reply. Nature wanted it so, and it would be a crime to stifle its voice. The man can be audacious, such is his vocation;* someone has to declare. But every woman without chasteness is guilty and depraved, because she tramples on a sentiment natural to her sex.

How can one dispute the truth of this sentiment? If the whole earth did not give unmistakable witness to it, the simple compari-

* We must distinguish between this audacity, and insolence and brutality. For nothing issues from more opposed sentiments, nor does anything have more contrary effects. I suppose an innocent and free love, receiving its laws only from itself; it belongs to this love alone to preside at its mysteries and to form the union of persons as well as that of hearts. When a man insults the chasteness of woman and attacks with violence the charms of a young object which feels nothing for him, his coarseness is not the result of ardent passion; it is only scandalous outrage; it bespeaks a soul without morals [manners], without refinement, incapable of either love or decency. The greatest value of the pleasures is in the heart of the one who grants them; a true lover would find only pain, anger, and despair in the very possession of the one he loves if he thought he were not loved in return.

To wish to satisfy his desires insolently, without the consent of the one who gave rise to them, is the audacity of a satyr; that of a man is to know how to give witness to them without displeasing, to make them attractive, to act in such a way that they be shared, to enslave the sentiments before attacking the person. It is not yet enough to be loved; desires shared do not alone give the right to satisfy them; the consent of the will is also needed. The heart accords in vain what the will refuses. The decent man and the lover holds back even when he could obtain what he wishes. To win this silent consent is to make use of all the violence permitted in love. To read it in the eyes, to see it in the ways in spite of the mouth's denial, that is the art of he who knows how to love. If he then completes his happiness, he is not brutal, he is decent. He does not insult chasteness; he respects it; he serves it. He leaves it the honor of still defending what it would have perhaps abandoned.

son of the sexes would suffice for recognizing it. Is it not nature which adorns young women with those features so sweet and which a little shame renders even more touching? Is it not nature which puts that timid and tender glance in their eyes which is resisted with such difficulty? Is it not nature which gives their complexion more lustre and their skin more delicacy so that a modest blush can be better perceived? Is it not nature which renders them apprehensive so that they flee, and feeble so that they succumb? To what end are they given a heart more sensitive to pity, in running less speed, a body less robust, a shorter stature, more delicate muscles, if nature had not destined them to let themselves be vanquished? Subjected to the indispositions of pregnancy and the pains of childbirth, should such an increase in labor exact a diminution of strength? But, to be reduced to this hard estate, they had to be strong enough to succumb only when they want to and feeble enough always to have a pretext for submitting. This is exactly the point at which nature has placed them.

Let us move from reasoning to experience. If chasteness were a prejudice of society and education, this sentiment ought to increase in places where more attention is paid to education and where the social laws are ceaselessly refined; it ought to be weaker wherever man has stayed closer to the primitive state. It is all to the contrary.* In our mountains, the women are timid and modest; a word makes them blush; they dare not raise their eyes to men, and keep silence before them. In the big cities, chasteness is ignoble and base. It is the only thing for which a well brought up woman would be ashamed. And the honor of having made a decent man blush belongs only to women of the best tone.

The argument drawn from the example of the beasts proves nothing and is not true. Man is not a dog or a wolf. It is only necessary in his species to establish the first relations of society to give to

* I expect the following objection: Savage women are not chaste, for they go naked? I answer that ours are even less so; for they are dressed. See the end of this essay on the subject of the Lacedaemonian maidens.

his sentiments a morality unknown to beasts. The animals have a heart and passions; but the holy image of the decent and the fair enters only the heart of man.

In spite of this, where was it learned that instinct never produces effects in animals similar to those that shame produces in men? I see proofs to the contrary every day. I see some animals hide themselves when satisfying certain needs, in order to keep a disagreeable object from the senses; I see them, instead of fleeing, eager to cover the vestiges afterwards. What is needed for these efforts to have an air of propriety and decency other than that they be taken by men? In their loves I see caprices, choices, and concerted refusals which come very close to following the maxim of exciting the passions by obstacles. At the very instant I write this, I have before my eyes an example which confirms it. Two young pigeons in the happy time of their first loves provide me with a picture very different from the stupid brutality ascribed to them by our supposed wise men. The white female goes following her beloved step by step and takes flight herself as soon as he turns around. Does he remain inactive? Light pecks with the bill wake him up; if he retires, he is pursued; if he protects himself, a little flight of six steps attracts him again. Nature's innocence arranges the provocations and the feeble resistance with an art which the most skillful coquette could hardly attain. No, the playful Galatea did not do better, and Virgil could have drawn one of his most charming images from a pigeon house.

Even if it could be denied that a special sentiment of chasteness was natural to women, would it be any the less true that in society their lot ought to be a domestic and retired life, and that they ought to be raised in principles appropriate to it? If the timidity, chasteness, and modesty which are proper to them are social inventions, it is in society's interest that women acquire these qualities; they must be cultivated in women, and any woman who disdains them offends good morals [manners]. Is there a sight in the world so touching, so respectable, as that of a mother surrounded by her children, directing the work of her domestics, procuring a happy life for her husband and prudently governing the home? It is here that she shows herself in all the dignity of a decent woman; it is here that she really commands respect, and beauty shares with honor the homages rendered to virtue. A home whose mistress is absent is a body without a soul which soon falls into corruption; a woman outside of her home loses her greatest luster, and, despoiled of her real ornaments, she displays herself indecently. If she has a husband, what is she seeking among men? If she does not, how can she expose herself to putting off, by an immodest bearing, he who might be tempted to become her husband? Whatever she may do, one feels that in public she is not in her place; and her very beauty, which pleases without attracting, is only one more fault for which the heart reproaches her. Whether this impression comes to us from nature or education, it is common to all the peoples of the world; everywhere, women are esteemed in proportion to their modesty; everywhere, there is the conviction that in neglecting the ways of their sex they neglect its duties; everywhere, it is seen that, when they take on the masculine and firm assurance of the man and turn it into effrontery, they abase themselves by this odious imitation and dishonor both their sex and ours.

I know that in some countries contrary customs prevail. But look at the sort of morals [manners] to which they have given rise. I need no other example to confirm my maxims. Let us apply to the morals [manners] of women what I said above concerning the honor with which they are treated. Among all the ancient civilized peoples they led very retired lives; they appeared rarely in public; never with men, they did not go walking with them; they did not have the best places at the theatre; they did not put themselves on display;* they were not even always permitted to go; and it is well

* In the Athenian theatre, the women occupied a high gallery called *Cercis*, neither convenient for seeing nor being seen; but it appears from the adventure of Valeria and Sulla[70] that at the Roman Circus they were mixed with the men.

THE LETTER TO M. D'ALEMBERT ON THE THEATRE

known that there was a death penalty for those who dared to show themselves at the Olympic games.

In the home, they had a private apartment where the men never entered. When their husbands entertained for dinner, they rarely presented themselves at the table; the decent women went out before the end of the meal, and the others never appeared at the beginning. There was no common place of assembly for the two sexes; they did not pass the day together. This effort not to become sated with one another made their meetings more pleasant. It is certain that domestic peace was, in general, better established and that greater harmony prevailed between man and wife* than is the case today.

Such were the practices of the Persians, the Greeks, the Romans, and even the Egyptians, in spite of Herodotus' bad jokes which refute themselves.[71] If, on occasion, women stepped out of the bounds of this modesty, the public outcry showed that this was an exception. What has not been said about the liberty of the fair sex at Sparta? It can also be seen in the *Lysistrata* of Aristophanes how shocking the impudence of the Athenian women was in the eyes of the Greeks; and, at Rome, already corrupted, with what scandal were the Roman ladies viewed who presented themselves at the tribunal of the triumvirs!

Everything is changed. Since then, hordes of barbarians, dragging their women with them in their armies, have inundated Europe; the licentiousness of camps, combined with the natural coldness of the northern climates, which makes reserve less necessary, introduced another way of life which was encouraged by the books of chivalry, in which beautiful ladies spent their lives in getting themselves honorably and decently kidnapped by men. Since these books were the schools of gallantry of the time, the libertine ideas that they inspire were introduced, especially at the courts and in

* The cause could be attributed to the facility of divorce; but the Greeks made little use of it, and Rome existed five hundred years before anyone took advantage of the law which permitted it.

the big cities where people pride themselves rather more on their refinement; by the very progress of this refinement, it had to degenerate finally into coarseness. It is thus that the modesty natural to women has little by little disappeared and that the manners [morals] of sutlers have been transmitted to women of quality.

But, do you want to know how shocking these practices, contrary to natural ideas, are for those who have not the habit of them? You can judge from the surprise and distress of foreigners and people from the provinces at the sight of these ways so new for them. This distress constitutes a praise of the women of their country, and it is to be believed that those who cause it would be less proud of it if its source were better known to them. It is not that this impresses, but rather that it embarrasses, and that chasteness, banished by the woman from her speech and her bearing, takes refuge in the heart of the man.

To return now to our actresses, I ask how an estate, the unique object of which is to show oneself off to the public and, what is worse, for money, could agree with decent women and be compatible with modesty and good morals [manners]? Is there even need to dispute about the moral differences between the sexes to feel how unlikely it is that she who sets herself for sale in performance would not soon do the same in person and never let herself be tempted to satisfy desires that she takes so much effort to excite? What! In spite of countless timid precautions, a decent and prudent woman, exposed to the least danger, has nevertheless great difficulty in keeping a faithful heart; and these audacious young persons, with no education other than in a system of coquetterie and amorous roles, immodestly dressed,* constantly surrounded by ardent and daring youth, in the midst of the sweet voices of love and pleasure—these young persons, I say, will resist their age, their heart, the objects that surround them, the speeches addressed to them, the ever recurring opportunities, and the gold for which

* What shall we say if we assume that they possess the beauty which is usually expected of them? See the *Entretiens sur le Fils naturel.*[72]

they are beforehand half sold! We would have to be believed to possess a childlike simplicity for someone to want to impose on us to this extent. Vice in vain hides itself in obscurity; its imprint is on the guilty faces. A woman's audacity is the sure sign of her shame; it is for having too much cause to blush that she blushes no more; and, if chasteness sometimes outlives purity, what must one think about purity when chasteness itself is extinguished?

Let us assume, if you wish, that there have been some exceptions; let us assmue:

> that there are as many as three whom one could name.[73]

I am prepared to believe what I have never seen nor head said. But shall we call a profession decent in which a decent woman is a prodigy and which leads us to despise those who exercise it unless we count on a constant miracle? Immodesty conforms so well to their estate and they are so well aware of it themselves that there is not one who would not think herself ridiculous even in feigning to take for her own the discourses of prudence and honor that she retails to the public. For fear that these severe maxims might make a progress injurious to her interests, the actress is always the first to parody her role and destroy her own work. As soon as she reaches the wings, she divests herself of the morality of the theatre as well as of her dignity; and if lessons of virtue are learned on the stage, they are quickly forgotten in the dressing rooms.

After what I have just said, I believe I need not explain further how the dissoluteness of the actresses leads to that of the actors; especially in a profession which forces them to live in the greatest familiarity with each other. I need not show how, from an estate which dishonors, indecent sentiments arise, nor how the vices divide those whom common interest ought to unite. I shall not expand on the countless subjects for discord and quarrels which the distribution of roles, the division of the receipts, the choice of plays, and the jealousy over applause must constantly excite, principally among the actresses, not to speak of the intrigues of gallantry. It is even more useless that I set forth the effects that the association of luxury and misery, inevitable among this sort of person, must naturally produce. I have already said too much for you and for reasonable men; I could never say enough for the predisposed who do not want to see what reason shows them but only what accords with their passions or their prejudices.

If all this is bound up with the actor's profession, what shall we do, Sir, to prevent its inevitable effects? As for me, I see only one way; it is to remove the cause. When the ills of a man come to him from his nature or a certain way of life which he cannot change, do the doctors try to prevent them? To forbid an actor to be vicious is to forbid the man to be sick.

Does it follow from this that we must despise all actors? On the contrary, it follows that an actor who is modest, decent, and has morals [manners] is, as you have said so well, doubly estimable, since he shows thereby that his love of virtue wins out over the passions of man and the ascendency of his profession. The only fault that can be imputed to him is to have chosen it in the first place; but, too often, a youthful error decides life's destiny; and when a man feels a real talent in himself, can he resist its appeal? The great actors carry their excuse with them; it is the bad ones who ought to be despised.

IX

If I have stayed so long with the terms of the general proposition, it is not that I would not have had even more advantage in applying it directly to the city of Geneva; but repugnance to putting my fellow citizens on the stage has caused me to put off speaking of us as long as I could. However, I must come to it at last; and I would have fulfilled my task only imperfectly if I did not seek to establish what will result in our particular situation from the founding of a theatre in our city if your opinion and your reasons determine the government to tolerate one there. I shall limit myself to effects so evident that they could not be contested by anyone who knows a bit about our constitution.

Geneva is rich, it is true; but although those enormous disproportions of fortune, which impoverish a whole land to enrich a few inhabitants and sow misery around opulence, are not to be seen there, it is certain that, if some Genevans possess a rather large property, many live in relatively harsh poverty and that the easy circumstances of the majority come from hard work, economy, and moderation rather than positive wealth. There are many cities poorer than our own in which the citizen can give much more to his pleasures because the land which feeds him is never worn out, and, since his time is of no value, he can waste it without loss. It is not so with us, who, without lands to subsist by, have only our industry. The people of Geneva supports itself only by dint of labor and has what is necessary only insofar as it denies itself every excess; this is one of the reasons for our sumptuary laws. It seems to me that what ought first to strike every foreigner coming to Geneva is the air of life and activity which prevails there. Everyone is busy, everyone is moving, everyone is about his work and his affairs. I do not believe that any other city so small in the world presents such a spectacle. Visit the St. Gervais Quarter. All the watchmaking of Europe seems centered there. Go through the Molard and the low streets; there, an organization for commerce on a large scale, stacks of boxes, barrels scattered at random, an odor of the orient and of spices, make you think you are in a seaport. At Paquis and Eaux-Vives the sight and sound of the printed calico and linen mills seems to transport you to Zurich. The city appears, as it were, multiplied by the labors which take place in it; and I have seen people who, at first glance, estimate the population at a hundred thousand souls. Its aims, its use of time, its vigilance, its austere parsimony, are the treasures of Geneva. This is with what we await an amusement of the idle which, in taking from us both time and money, will truly double our loss.

Geneva does not have twenty-four thousand inhabitants, you

will agree. I see that Lyons, much richer in proportion, and at least five or six times more populous, barely supports a theatre and that, if this theatre were an opera, the city would not be adequate to it. I see that Paris, the capital of France and the whirlpool which engulfs the wealth of this great realm, supports three in what is at best a modest fashion, and a fourth at certain seasons of the year. Let us suppose that this fourth* were permanent. I see that with more than six hundred thousand inhabitants, this meeting place of opulence and idleness provides, all things considered, scarcely one thousand to twelve hundred spectators daily. In the rest of the realm, I see that Bordeaux, Rouen, large seaports, I see that Lille, Strasbourg, large military centers, full of idle officers who spend their lives waiting for noon and eight o'clock, have each a dramatic theatre; yet involuntary taxes are needed to support it. But how many other cities incomparably larger than ours, how many seats of both royal and autonomous courts of justice, cannot support a resident theatre.

In order to judge if we are in a position to do better, let us take a well-known point of comparison, such as, for example, Paris. I say, then, that, if more than six hundred thousand inhabitants provide, altogether, only twelve hundred spectators daily for the Paris theatres, less than twenty-four thousand inhabitants will certainly not provide more than forty-eight at Geneva. Moreover, free tickets must be deducted from this number, and it must be supposed that there are not proportionally fewer unoccupied people at Geneva than at Paris, a supposition that seems to me indefensible.

Now, if the actors of the French theatre, pensioned by the king and proprietors of their own theatre, have great difficulty in

* If I do not count the concerts of religious music, it is because, rather than being a theatrical entertainment added to the others, they are only a supplement to them. I do not count the little shows at the fair either; but I count the theatre there for the whole year, while it only lasts six months. In investigating by comparison whether it is possible for a troop to exist in Geneva, I suppose, everywhere, relations more favorable to the affirmative than the known facts warrant.

supporting themselves at Paris with an audience of three hundred spectators per performance,* I ask how the actors of Geneva will support themselves with an audience of forty-eight spectators for their entire resource? You will tell me that life is cheaper in Geneva than in Paris. Yes, but the tickets will cost proportionately less; and then, board is nothing for actors. It is costumes and jewelry which cost. All this must be sent for from Paris or maladroit workers must be trained. It is in places where all these things are common that they are most cheaply made. You will say that they will be subjected to our sumptuary laws. But we would wish in vain to bring reform to the theatre; never will Cleopatra or Xerxes have a taste for our simplicity. Since the business of actors is to appear, it is to deprive them of the taste for their craft to prevent them from appearing; and I doubt if ever a good actor would consent to becoming a Quaker. Finally, it can be objected that the Geneva troop, since it will be considerably less numerous than that of Paris, will be able to subsist at considerably less cost. Agreed; but will this difference be in the proportion of 48 to 300? Add that a more numerous company has also the advantage of being able to play more often, while in a little company, which lacks understudies, not everyone can play every day; the illness or the absence of a single actor causes a performance to be missed, and this means that much lost for the receipts.

The Genevans are excessively fond of the country; this can be judged by the number of homes scattered out around the city. The charm of the hunt and the beauty of the surroundings nourish this salutary taste. The gates, closed before nightfall, deprive one of the liberty of taking walks outside; and, since the country homes are so near, very few well-to-do people sleep in town during the summer. Each, having spent the day at his business, leaves at

* Those who only go to the theatre on nice days, when the audience is large, will find this estimate too low; but those who have followed it for ten years, as I have, good and bad days alike, will certainly find it too high.

If, then, we must reduce the daily number of three hundred at Paris, we must reduce that of forty-eight at Geneva, which strengthens my objections.

the closing of the gates in the evening and goes to his little retreat
to breathe the purer air and enjoy the most charming countryside
on earth. There are even many citizens and townsmen who reside
there the whole year and have no dwelling in Geneva. All of this is
so much lost to the theatre; and, during the entire season of good
weather, almost the only ones remaining to support it will be
people who never go. In Paris it is an entirely different thing; there
one can combine the theatre and the country quite well; and, during
the whole summer, you see nothing but carriages leaving the gates
of the city at the hour when the theatre is over. As to the people
who sleep in town, the liberty of going out at any time tempts them
less than the inconveniences which accompany it repel them. One
gets bored so quickly with the public walks, one must go so far to
find the country, its air is so infected with filth, and the prospect is
so unattractive, that it is preferable to go and close oneself up in
the theatre. Here is another difference to the disadvantage of our
actors, and a half of the year lost for them. Do you think, Sir, that
they will easily find in the remainder enough to fill up such a large
void? As for me, I see no other remedy than that of changing the
hour at which the gates are closed, of sacrificing our security to
our pleasures and leaving a fortress open nights,* in the midst of
three powers of which the furthest removed has to go only half a
league to come up to our glacis.

This is not all; it is impossible that an establishment so contrary
to our ancient maxims be generally applauded. How many generous
citizens will look on with indignation at this monument of luxury
and softness being elevated on the ruins of our antique simplicity
and threatening from afar the public liberty? Do you think that

* I know that all our great fortifications are the most useless thing in the
world, and that, even if we had enough troops to defend them, they would
still be quite useless; for surely no one would come to besiege us. But, because
we have no siege to fear, we ought no less to be on the lookout to guarantee
ourselves against every surprise; nothing is so easy as to assemble troops in
our neighborhood. We have learned the use that can be made of this only too
well, and we ought to recognize that the rights that are least founded for those
who are outside of a city turn out to be excellent when they are inside of it.[74]

they will go to lend their authority to this innovation by their presence after having openly disapproved of it? Be certain that many go to the theatre in Paris without scruple who will never set foot in it in Geneva because the good of their country is dearer to them than their amusement. Where will the imprudent mother be who will dare to take her daughter to this dangerous school? And how many respectable women will think that they are disgracing themselves in going? If in Paris some persons abstain from going to the theatre, it is solely from religious principle, which will surely be no less strong among us; and we will have more motives of morals [manners], of virtue, and of patriotism which will restrain even those whom religion would not.*

I have shown that it is absolutely impossible to support a theatre at Geneva with the sole participation of the spectators. One of two things is necessary then: either the rich must subscribe to support it, a heavy burden which they will surely not be disposed to bear for a long time; or the state must involve itself and support the theatre at its own expense. But how will the state support the theatre? If it be by cutting back on the necessary expenses, for which its modest revenue barely suffices, with what will these be provided? Or, for this important use, will it destine the sums which economy and the integrity of the administration sometimes permit to be put in reserve for the most pressing needs? Must we discharge our little garrison and guard our gates ourselves? Must we reduce the slender honoraria of our magistrates, or shall we deprive ourselves for this purpose of every resource for the least unforeseen accident? Without these expedients, I see only one which is practicable; that is the way of taxes and assessments, which means to assemble our citizens and townsmen in general council in the

* I do not mean by this that one can be virtuous without religion; I held this erroneous opinion for a long time, but now I am only too disabused. But I mean that a believer can sometimes, from motives of purely social virtue, abstain from certain actions, indifferent in themselves and which do not immediately involve the conscience, such as going to the theatre in a place where it is not good to tolerate it.

temple of St. Pierre and there solemnly to propose that a tax be accorded for the establishment of the theatre.[75] God forbid that I should believe our wise and worthy magistrates capable of ever making such a proposal; and from your own article one can judge how it would be received.

If we had the misfortune of finding some expedient adequate to overcoming these difficulties, it would be so much the worse for us; for that could come to pass only by means of some secret vice which, in weakening us still more in our smallness, would sooner or later destroy us. Let us suppose, nevertheless, that a noble zeal for the theatre accomplished a miracle of this order; let us suppose the actors well established in Geneva, well controlled by our laws, the drama flourishing and frequented. Finally, let us suppose that our city has attained the situation of which you speak, that is, with both theatre and morals [manners] it would combine the advantages of both, advantages, moreover, which are, as far as I can see, hardly compatible, since the advantage of the theatre, which is to supplement morals [manners], is of no account where morals [manners] exist.

The first noticeable effect of this establishment will be, as I have already said, a revolution in our practices which will necessarily produce one in our morals [manners]. Will this revolution be good or bad? It is time to examine this.

There is no well-constituted state in which practices are not to be found which are linked to the form of government and which help to preserve it. The clubs in London were institutions of this sort before they were so unseasonably ridiculed by the authors of the *Spectator;* to these clubs, thus become ridiculous, have succeeded the coffee houses and the houses of ill fame. I doubt if the English people has gained much in the exchange. Similar clubs are now established in Geneva under the name of *circles;* and I have reason, Sir, to judge from your article that you did not observe without esteem the tone of good sense and judgment which they cause to prevail there. This practice is old among us although its name is not. The clubs existed in my childhood under the name of societies; but their form was not so good nor so regular. The exercise of arms which brings us together every spring, the various prizes which are awarded during one part of the year, the military festivals which these prizes occasion, the taste for the hunt common to all the Genevans, bringing the men frequently together, gave them the occasion to form among themselves dining societies, country outings and, finally, bonds of friendship. But these assemblies, having for their object only pleasures and joy, were pretty much always formed in taverns. Our civil discords, during which the necessity of affairs obliged us to meet more often and to deliberate coldly and calmly, caused these tumultuous societies to be changed into more decent associations. These associations took the name of *circles* and, from a very sad cause, issued very good effects.*

These *circles* are societies of twelve to fifteen persons who rent comfortable quarters which they provide with furniture and the necessary store at common expense. Every afternoon all the associates whose affairs or pleasures do not retain them elsewhere go to these quarters. They meet and there each gives himself without restraint to the amusements of his taste; they gamble, chat, read, drink and smoke. Sometimes they dine there, but rarely, because the Genevan is a steady sort and likes to live with his family. Also, they often go walking together, and the amusements they provide for themselves are exercises fit to cause and maintain a robust body. The women and the girls, for their part, meet in societies at one another's homes. The object of this meeting is to provide the occasion for a little social card-playing, refreshments, and, as can be imagined, inexhaustible gossiping. The men, without being very severely excluded from these societies, are rather rarely involved in them; and I should think even worse of those who are always to be found there than of those who never are.

Such are the daily amusements of the Geneva townsmen. Not unendowed with pleasure and gaiety, these amusements have

* I shall speak hereafter of the disadvantages.

something simple and innocent which suits republican morals [manners]; but the moment there is drama, goodby to the *circles*, goodby to the societies! This is the revolution I predicted; all of this necessarily decays, and if you object the example of London cited by me where the established theatre did not prevent the clubs, I shall answer that there is, in relation to us, an extreme difference; it is that a theatre, which is only a speck in that immense city, will be in ours a great object which will absorb everything.

If you ask me next what is so bad about abolishing the *circles* . . . , No, Sir, that question will not come from a philosopher; it is a woman's speech, or that of a young man who treats our *circles* as guardhouses and thinks he smells the odor of tobacco. I must nevertheless answer; for, this once, although I address myself to you, I write for the people, and doubtless it is clear that I do so; but you have forced me to it.

I say, in the first place, that, if the odor of tobacco is a bad thing, it is a very good one to remain the master of one's property and to be sure of sleeping at home. But I am already forgetting that I do not write for d'Alemberts. I must express myself in another way.

Let us follow the indications of nature, let us consult the good of society; we shall find that the two sexes ought to come together sometimes and to live separated ordinarily. I said it before concerning women, I say it now concerning men. They are affected as much as, and more than, women by a commerce that is too intimate; they lose not only their morals [manners], but we lose our morals [manners] and our constitution; for this weaker sex, not in the position to take on our way of life, which is too hard for it, forces us to take on its way, too soft for us; and, no longer wishing to tolerate separation, unable to make themselves into men, the women make us into women.

This disadvantageous result which degrades man is very important everywhere; but it is especially so in states like ours, whose interest it is to prevent it. Whether a monarch governs men or women ought to be rather indifferent to him, provided that he be obeyed; but in a republic, men are needed.*

The ancients spent almost their whole lives in the open air, either dispatching their business or taking care of the state's in the public place, or walking in the country, in gardens, on the seashore, in the rain or under the sun, and almost always bareheaded.** In all of this, no women; but they were quite able to find them in case of need, and we do not find from their writings and the samples of their conversation which are left to us that intelligence, taste, or even love, lost anything by this reserve. As for us, we have taken on entirely contrary ways; meanly devoted to the wills of the sex which we ought to protect and not serve, we have learned to despise it in obeying it, to insult it by our derisive attentions; and every woman at Paris gathers in her apartment a harem of men more womanish than she, who know how to render all sorts of homage to beauty except that of the heart, which is her due. But observe these same men, always constrained in these voluntary prisons, get up, sit down, pace continually back and forth to the fireplace, to the window, pick up and set down a fan a hundred times, leaf through books, glance at pictures, turn and pirouette about the room, while the idol, stretched out motionlessly on her couch, has only her eyes and her tongue active. From where does this difference come if it is not that nature, which imposes this sed-

* I will be told that kings need men for war. Not at all. Instead of thirty thousand men, they need, for example, only raise one hundred thousand women. Women do not lack courage; they prefer honor to life; when they fight, they fight well. The difficulty with their sex is its not being able to support the fatigues of war and the intemperance of the seasons. The secret is, hence, always to have triple the number which is necessary for fighting in order to sacrifice the other two-thirds to sickness and mortality.

Who would believe that this joke, the application of which can be seen easily enough, should have been taken literally in France by some intelligent people.[76]

** After the battle won by Cambyses over Psammenitus, the Egyptians, who always went bareheaded, were distinguished among the dead by the extreme hardness of their skulls, while the Persians, always wearing their big tiaras, had skulls so tender that they could be broken without effort. Herodotus himself bore witness to this difference a long time afterwards.[77]

entary and homebound life on women, prescribes an entirely opposite one for men, and that this restlessness indicates a real need in
them? If the Orientals, whose warm climate causes them to sweat
a good deal, do little exercise and do not go walking at all, at least
they go and sit in the open air and breath at their ease, while here
the women take great pains to suffocate their friends in sound
rooms well closed.

If the strength of the men of antiquity is compared to that of
the men of today, no sort of equality can be found. Our gentlemen's exercises are children's games next to those of ancient gym-
nastic; rackets (*la paume*) has been abandoned as too fatiguing,
and we can no longer travel by horseback. I say nothing of our
troops. The marches of the Greek and Roman armies can no longer
be conceived. Just to read of the length of march, the work, and
the burden of the Roman soldier is tiring and overwhelms the
imagination. Horses were not permitted to the infantry officers.
Often the generals made the same journeys on foot that their troops
did. Never did the two Catos travel otherwise, either alone or with
their armies. Otho himself, the effeminate Otho, marched in full
armor at the head of his army in going to meet Vitellius. Let one
fighting man be found today capable of doing as much. We are
fallen in everything. Our painters and sculptors complain about
not being able to find models comparable to those of antique art
anymore. Why is that? Has man degenerated? Has the species a
physical decrepitude just as does the individual? On the contrary;
the northern barbarians, who have, so to speak, peopled Europe
with a new race, were bigger and stronger than the Romans whom
they vanquished and subjugated. We ought then to be stronger
ourselves, we who for the most part are descended from these
newcomers; but the first Romans lived like men* and found in their

* The Romans were the smallest and weakest men of all the peoples of
Italy; and this difference was so great, says Livy, that it was noticeable at first
glance in the troops of both. Nevertheless, exercise and discipline prevailed
so much over nature that the weak did what the strong could not do and
vanquished them.[78]

constant exercises the vigor that nature had refused them, while we lose ours in the indolent and soft life to which our dependence on women reduces us. If the barbarians of whom I have just spoken lived with women, they did not, for all that, live like them. It was they who had the courage to live like the men, just as the Spartan women did. The woman made herself robust, and the man was not enervated.

If this effort to oppose Nature is hurtful to the body, it is even more so to the mind. Imagine what can be the temper of the soul of a man who is uniquely occupied with the important business of amusing women, and who spends his entire life doing for them what they ought to do for us when, exhausted by labors of which they are incapable, our minds have need of relaxation. Given to these puerile habits, to what that is great could we ever raise ourselves? Our talents and our writings savor of our frivolous occupations;* agreeable if one wishes, but, small and cold like our sentiments, they have as their sole merit that easy and clever style which is not hard to give to nothings. These throngs of ephemeral works which come to light every day, made only to amuse women and having neither strength nor depth, fly from the dressing table to the counter.[79] This is the way to rewrite ever again the same things and to make them always new. Two or three will be cited which will serve as exceptions; but I will cite a hundred thousand which

* Women, in general, do not like any art, know nothing about any, and have no genius. They can succeed in little works which require only quick wit, taste, grace, and sometimes even a bit of philosophy and reasoning. They can acquire science, erudition, talents, and everything which is acquired by dint of work. But that celestial flame which warms and sets fire to the soul, that genius which consumes and devours, that burning eloquence, those sublime transports which carry their raptures to the depths of hearts, will always lack in the writings of women; their works are all cold and pretty as they are; they may contain as much wit as you please, never a soul; they are a hundred times more sensible than passionate. They do not know how to describe nor to feel even love. Only Sappho, as far as I know, and one other woman, deserve to be excepted. I would bet anything in the world that the *Lettres portugaises* were written by a man. Now, everywhere that women dominate, their taste must also dominate; and this is what determines the taste of our age.

will confirm the rule. It is for this reason that most of the productions of our age will pass with it, and posterity will think that very few books were written in this age which produced so many.

It would not be hard to show that instead of gaining by these practices, the women lose. They are flattered without being loved; they are served without being honored; they are surrounded by agreeable persons but they no longer have lovers; and the worst is that the former, without having the sentiments of the latter, usurp nonetheless all the rights. The society of the two sexes, having become too usual and too easy, has produced these two effects, and it is thus that the general spirit of gallantry stifles both genius and love.

As for me, I find it hard to conceive how men can honor women so little as to dare to address these stale amorous speeches ceaselessly to them, these insulting and mocking compliments to which they do not even deign to give an air of good faith. When we insult women by these evident lies, does it not amount to declaring to them rather plainly that no obliging truth can be found to say to them? It happens only too often that love makes illusions for itself about the qualities of the one who is loved; but is there a question of love in all this tedious jargon? Do not all those who use it use it equally for all women? And would they not be vexed if they were thought to be seriously in love with a single one? Let them not be disquieted. It would require strange ideas of love to believe them capable of it, and nothing is so far removed from its tone than that of gallantry. In the way that I conceive of this terrible passion, its perplexity, its frenzies, its palpitations, its transports, its burning expressions, its even more energetic silence, its inexpressible looks which their timidity renders reckless and which give evidence of desires through fear, it seems to me that, after a language so vehement, if the lover only once brought himself to say, "I love you," the beloved, outraged, would say to him, "you do not love me anymore," and would never see him again in her life.

Our *circles* still preserve some image of ancient morals [manners] among us. By themselves, the men, exempted from having to lower their ideas to the range of women and to clothe reason in gallantry, can devote themselves to grave and serious discourse without fear of ridicule. They dare to speak of country and virtue without passing for windbags; they even dare to be themselves without being enslaved to the maxims of a magpie. If the turn of conversation becomes less polished, reasons take on more weight; they are not satisfied by jokes or compliments. They cannot get away with fine phrases for answers. They do not humor one another in dispute; each, feeling himself attacked by all the forces of his adversary, is obliged to use all his own to defend himself; it is thus that the mind gains precision and vigor. If some licentious remarks are mixed in with all this, one ought not to take umbrage at it. The least vulgar are not always the most decent, and this language, a bit rustic, is still preferable to the more studied style with which the two sexes mutually seduce one another and familiarize themselves in all propriety with vice. The way of life that is more in conformity with the inclinations of man is also better suited to his temperament. He does not remain settled in a chair for the whole day. He applies himself to games which give exercise, he comes and goes; many *circles* are held in the country, others go there. There are gardens for walking, spacious courts for exercise, a big lake for swimming, the whole country is open for the hunt. And it must not be thought that this hunt is conducted so comfortably as in the environs of Paris, where game is to be found underfoot and where one can shoot on horseback. In a word, these decent and innocent institutions combine everything which can contribute to making friends, citizens, and soldiers out of the same men, and, in consequence, everything which is most appropriate to a free people.

The societies of women are blamed for one failing; they make the women scandalmongers and satirists; and, indeed, one can easily understand that the anecdotes of a little city do not escape these feminine meetings; it can also be believed that the absent husbands are hardly spared; and no pretty and sought-after woman has an easy time of it in her neighbor's *circle*. But perhaps there is more good than bad in this failing, and it is, in any event, incontestably less harmful than those whose place it takes; for which is better, that a woman speak ill of her husband with her friends or that she do it with a man in private conversation, that she criticize the disorder of her neighbor or that she imitate it? Although the Genevans tell rather easily what they know and sometimes what they conjecture, they are really disgusted by calumny, and they will never be heard to make accusations against another that they believe to be false; while in other countries, the women, guilty equally by their silence and by their speech, hide, for fear of reprisals, the ill which they know, and publish for vengeance what they have invented.

How many public scandals are prevented for fear of these severe observers? They almost perform the function of censors in our city. It is thus that in the great days of Rome, the citizens, watching one another, publicly accused one another out of zeal for justice; but when Rome was corrupted and there was nothing left to do for good morals [manners] other than to hide the bad ones, the hatred of vices which unmasks them became one itself. The infamous informers succeeded zealous citizens; and, whereas formerly the good accused the vicious, they were accused in their turn. Thank heaven we are far from so terrible an end. We are not reduced to hiding from our own eyes for fear of disgusting ourselves. As for me, I will not have a better opinion of women when they are more circumspect. Women will humor one another more when there are more reasons for doing so and when each will need for herself the discretion the example of which she will set for others.

So then, we need not be much disturbed by the cackle of the women's societies. Let them speak ill of others so much as they like, provided they do so among themselves. Really corrupt women could not long endure this way of life; and, however dear gossip may be to them, they would want to gossip with men. No matter what people have said to me about them, I have never seen any of these societies without a secret sentiment of esteem and respect for those who compose them. Such is, I said to myself, the plan of nature, which gives different tastes to the two sexes, so that they live apart and each in his way.* Thus, these agreeable persons spend all their days devoted to occupations which are suitable for them or to innocent and simple amusements, quite apt to move a decent heart and to give a good opinion of them. I do not know what they said but they lived together; they may have spoken of men but they did without them; and, although they criticized the conduct of others so severely, at least their own was irreproachable.

The *circles* of men doubtlessly also have their disadvantages; what that is human does not? They gamble, they drink, they get drunk, they spend the whole night; all this may be true, all this may be exaggerated. There is everywhere a mixture of good and evil, but in different degrees. Everything is abused, a trivial axiom on the basis of which one ought neither to reject everything nor to accept everything. The rule for choosing is simple. When the good surpasses the evil, the thing ought to be accepted in spite of its disadvantages; when the evil surpasses the good, it must be rejected even with its advantages. When the thing is good in itself and bad only in its abuses, when the abuses can be provided against without much effort or tolerated without great harm, they can serve as the pretext, but not as the reason, for abolishing a useful practice; but what is bad in itself will always be bad,** whatever

* This principle, on which all good morals [manners] depend, is developed in a clearer and more extended way in a manuscript which I am now holding and which I propose to publish, if enough time remains for that, although this announcement is hardly fit for winning in advance the favor of ladies.

It will be easily understood that the manuscript about which I spoke in this note was the *Nouvelle Heloise*, which appeared two years after this work.[80]

** I speak of the moral order: for in the physical order there is nothing absolutely bad. The whole is good.

may be done to make good use of it. Such is the essential difference between the *circles* and the theatre.

The citizens of the same state, the inhabitants of the same city, are not anchorites; they could not always live alone and separated; if they could, it would not be necessary to constrain them to it. It is only the fiercest despotism which is alarmed at the sight of seven or eight men assembled, ever fearing that their conversation turns on their miseries.

Now, of all the kinds of relations which can bring individuals together in a city like our own, the *circles* form incontestably the most reasonable, the most decent, and the least dangerous ones, because they neither wish nor are able to be hidden, because they are public and permitted, because order and rule prevail in them. It is even easy to demonstrate that the abuses which might result from them would arise equally in all of the others or that they would produce even greater ones. Before thinking of destroying an established practice, those that will be introduced in its place ought to have been carefully weighed. Whoever can propose one which is feasible and from which no abuse will result, let him propose it, and after that the *circles* can be abolished; well and good. Meanwhile, let us, if need be, permit men to spend the night drinking who, without that, might spend it doing worse.

All intemperance is vicious, and especially the one which deprives us of the noblest of our faculties. The excess of wine degrades man, at the least alienates his reason for a time, and in the long run, brutalizes it. But, after all, the taste for wine is not a crime and rarely causes one to be committed; it makes man stupid, not evil.* For every fleeting quarrel that it causes, it forms a hundred durable attachments. Speaking generally, drinkers are cordial and

---

* Let us not calumniate the vice; is this not sufficiently achieved by its ugliness? Wine does not make wickedness, it only discloses wickedness. He who killed Clitus in drunkenness, slew Philotas in cold blood. If drunkenness has its furies, what passion does not? The difference is that the others subsist deep in the soul, while this one takes fire and is extinguished instantaneously. Apart from this outburst, which passes and can easily be avoided, we can be sure that whoever does evil deeds in wine is hatching evil plots when sober.

frank; they are almost all good, upright, just, faithful, brave, and decent men except for their single failing. Would one dare to say as much for the vices that are substituted for this one? Or can one pretend to make out of a whole city a race of men without failings, and self-controlled in everything? How many apparent virtues often hide real vices! The wise man is sober by temperance, the cheat out of hypocrisy. In the countries of bad morals [manners], intrigues, treason, and adultery, men are apprehensive about an indiscreet state in which the heart is revealed while we are not on our guard. Everywhere, the people who most abhor drunkenness are those for whom it is most important to protect themselves from it. In Switzerland it is almost esteemed, in Naples it is detested. But, in the final accounting, which is more to be feared, the intemperance of the Swiss or the reserve of the Italian?

I repeat, it would be better to be sober and true, not only for oneself but even for society; for everything which is bad in morality is also bad in politics. But the preacher stops at personal evil, the magistrate sees only the public consequences; the former has as his object only man's perfection, to which man never attains; the latter, only the good of the state insofar as it can be attained; thus all that it is right to blame from the pulpit ought not to be punished by the laws. Never has a people perished from an excess of wine; all perish from the disorder of women. The reason for this difference is clear; the first of these two vices turns one away from the others; the second engenders them all. The diversity of ages has something to do with it too. Wine tempts youth less and drags it down less easily; hot blood gives it other desires; in the age of passions all are inflamed by the fire of a single one, reason is perverted at its birth, and man, still untamed, becomes undisciplinable before having borne the yoke of the laws. But let half-chilled blood seek a support which reanimates it, let a beneficent liquor take the place of the spirits that it has no more;* when an

* Plato, in his *Laws*, permits the use of wine only to the old men, and he sometimes even permits them its excess.

old man abuses this sweet remedy, he has already fulfilled his duties to his country; he deprives it only of the refuse of his years. He is at fault no doubt; he ceases to be a citizen before his death. But the other has not even begun being one; he makes himself, rather, into a public enemy by the seduction of his accomplices, by the example of the effect of his corrupted morals [manners] and, above all, by the pernicious moral principles he cannot fail to disseminate in order to authorize his deeds. It would have been better had he never existed.

From the passion for gambling arises a more dangerous abuse, but one that can be easily provided against or repressed. This is an affair for the police, the inspection of which is easier and more becoming in the *circles* than in private homes. Opinion can do much on this point; and as soon as the games that involve exercise and skill are made honorable, cards, dice, and games of chance will inevitably fall in decay. I do not even believe, whatever may be said, that these idle and delusive means of filling one's purse ever gain much credit with a reasonable and hard-working people, which knows too well the value of time and money to like losing them together.

Let us then preserve the *circles*, even with their faults. For these faults are not in the *circles* but in the men who compose them; and there is no imaginable form of social life in which the same faults do not produce more harmful effects. Again, let us not seek for the chimaera of perfection but for the best possible according to the nature of man and the constitution of society. There are some peoples to whom I would say, destroy your circles and clubs, remove every barrier of propriety between the two sexes; ascend again, if it is possible, to the point of being only corrupt. But you, Genevans, avoid becoming corrupt if there is still time. Beware of the first step which is never the last one, and consider that it is easier to keep good morals [manners] than to put an end to bad ones.

Only two years of theater and everything will be overturned.

They could not possibly divide themselves among so many amusements; the hour of the theatre, being that of the *circles*, will cause them to dissolve; too many of the members will break away; those who remain will not be assiduous enough to be a great resource to one another nor to allow the associations to subsist for long. The two sexes meeting daily in the same place; the groups which will be formed for going there; the ways of life that they will see depicted in the theatre, which they will be eager to imitate; the exposition of the ladies and the maidens all tricked out in their very best and put on display in the boxes as though they were in the window of a shop waiting for buyers; the affluence of the handsome young who will come to show themselves off, for their part, and who will soon find it much nicer to caper in the theatre than to exercise on the Plain-Palais; the little suppers with women which will be arranged on leaving, even if they are only with the actresses; finally, the contempt for the old practices which will result from the adoption of the new ones, all of this will soon put the agreeable life of Paris and the fine airs of France in the place of our old simplicity; and I rather doubt that Parisians in Geneva will long preserve the taste for our government.

One must not dissemble; the intentions are still upright, but the morals [manners] already noticeably incline toward decadence, and we follow, at a distance, in the tracks of those same peoples whose fate does not fail to cause us anxiety. For example, I am told that the education of the young is generally much better than it was formerly; however, this can be proved only by showing that it makes better citizens. It is certain that the children know how to bow better, that they know how to offer their hand more gallantly to ladies and to say an infinity of charming things to them for which I would have them beaten, that they know how to make decisions, settle things, interrupt grown men, and pester everybody without modesty or discretion. I am told that this trains them; I agree that this trains them to be impertinent and that this is, of all the things they learn by this method, the only one

they do not forget. This is not all. In order to restrain them with
the women whom they are destined to divert, care is taken to
raise the children exactly like the women; they are protected from
the sun, the wind, the rain, and the dust so that they will never be
able to bear any of them. Since it is impossible to keep them from
all contact with air, things are at least arranged so that it only gets
to them after having lost half of its energy. They are deprived of
all exercise, they are relieved of all their faculties, and they are
rendered inept for any other activities than those to which they
are destined; the only thing which the women do not exact from
these vile slaves is that they consecrate themselves to their service
in the oriental fashion. With this difference, all that distinguishes
them from the women is that, since nature has refused them
women's graces, they substitute for them ridiculousness. On my
last trip to Geneva, I already saw several of these young ladies in
jerkins, with white teeth, plump hands, piping voices, and pretty
green parasols in their hands, rather maladroitly counterfeiting men.

Men were coarser in my time. The children, rustically raised,
had no complexion to preserve and did not fear the injuries of the
air to which they had been accustomed from an early date. The
fathers took the children with them on the hunt, in the country, to
all their exercises, in every society. Timid and modest before aged
people, they were hardy, proud, and quarrelsome among themselves. They had no hairdo to preserve; they challenged one another
at wrestling, running, and boxing. They fought in good earnest,
hurt one another sometimes, and then embraced in their tears. They
went home sweating, out of breath, and with their clothes torn;
they were real scamps, but these scamps made men who have zeal
for the service of the country in their hearts and blood to spill for
it. Please God that as much can be said one day for our fine little
spruced-up gentlemen and that these men of fifteen will not be
children of thirty.

Happily they are not all like this. The greater number still retain that old ruggedness which preserves a good constitution as

well as good morals [manners]. Even those whom an over-delicate education softens for a time will be constrained, when they are grown up, to bend themselves to the habits of their compatriots. The latter will lose their roughness in the commerce of the world; the former will gain strength in exercise; all will become, I hope, what their ancestors were, or, at least, what their fathers are today. But let us not flatter ourselves that we shall preserve our liberty in renouncing the morals [manners]which acquired it.

X

I RETURN to our actors, and, still supposing that they have a success which seems to me impossible, I find that this success will attack our constitution, not only in an indirect way, in attacking our morals [manners], but directly in disturbing the equilibrium which ought to prevail among the various parts of the state in order to preserve the whole body in good health.

From the many reasons that I could give, I shall content myself with choosing one which is most suitable for the greatest number, because it limits itself to considerations of self-interest and money, always more palpable to the vulgar than moral effects, of which they are unable to see either the connections with their causes, or their influence on the destiny of the state.

The theatre might be considered, if it succeeds, as a sort of tax which, although voluntary, is nonetheless onerous for the people in that it provides a continual occasion for expenditure which it cannot resist. This tax is a bad one, not only because none of it comes back to the sovereign, but especially because its distribution, far from being proportional, burdens the poor beyond their strength and relieves the rich in taking the place of the more costly amusements which they would provide for themselves for want of this one. To agree to this, one need only observe that the differences in the prices of the seats are not, nor can they be, in proportion to those of the fortunes of the people who fill them. At the *Comédie-Française*, the first boxes and the places on the stage are four francs ordinarily, and six on the days of special prices; the pit costs twenty sous; there have even been repeated attempts to increase it. Now, no one will say that the wealth of the richest who go to the theatre is only quadruple that of the poorest who sit in the pit. Speaking generally, the former are of an excessive opulence and most of the others have nothing.* It is with this as with the taxes on wheat, wine, salt, and everything necessary to life which have an appearance of justice at first glance and are at bottom very iniquitous; for the poor, who can only spend for necessities, are forced to throw away three quarters of what they spend in taxes, whereas, since the same necessities are only the least part of the expenditure of the rich, the tax is practically unnoticeable to them.** In this way, he who has little pays much, and he who has much pays little; I do not see what great justice can be found in that.

I will be asked who forces the poor to go to the theatre. I answer: first, those who establish it and give them the temptation. In the second place, their very poverty, which condemns them to constant labor without hope of seeing it end, makes some relaxation necessary for the poor in order to bear it. They do not consider themselves unhappy because they work without respite when

* Even if the difference in the prices of the seats were increased in proportion to those of the fortunes, the equilibrium would not be re-established as a result of that. These inferior seats, priced too low, would be abandoned to the populace; and everyone would always spend beyond his means to occupy more honorable ones. This is an observation that can be made at the shows in the fair. The reason for this disorder is that the first rows are then a fixed limit which the others can always approach without its being able to be moved farther away. The poor constantly tend to raise themselves above their twenty sous; but the rich, to flee them, have no asylum beyond their four francs; they must, in spite of themselves, let themselves be accosted and, if their pride suffers from it, their purse profits.

** This is why those, whom Bodin calls impostors,[81] and other public rascals, always establish their monopolies on the things necessary to life in order to starve the people gently without the rich grumbling. If the least object of luxury or ostentation were attacked, everything would be lost; but, provided the great are content, what difference does it make whether the people live?

everybody else does the same; but is it not cruel to the one who works to be deprived of the recreations of the idle? He shares them then; and this very amusement which provides a means of economy for the rich, doubly weakens the poor, either by a real increase in expenses or by less zeal for work, as I have explained it above.

From these new reflections, it follows evidently, I believe, that the modern theatre, which can only be attended for money, tends everywhere to promote and increase the inequality of fortunes, less noticeably, it is true, in the capitals than in a little city like our own. If I grant that this inequality, carried to a certain point, can have its advantages, you will certainly also grant that it ought to have limits, above all in a little state, above all in a republic. In a monarchy, where all the orders are intermediate between the prince and the people, it can be a matter of some indifference that certain men pass from one to the other; for since others replace them, this change does not interrupt the progression. But in a democracy, in which the subjects and the sovereign are only the same men considered in different relations, as soon as the smaller number wins out in riches over the greater number, the state must perish or change its form. Whether the rich become richer or the poor more indigent, the difference of fortunes is no less increased in one way than the other; and this difference, carried beyond its measure, is what destroys the equilibrium about which I have spoken.

Never in a monarchy can the opulence of an individual put him above the prince; but, in a republic, it can easily put him above the laws. Then the government no longer has force, and the rich are always the true sovereign. On the basis of these incontestable maxims, it remains to be considered whether inequality has not reached among us the last limit to which it can go without shaking the republic. I refer myself on this point to those who know our constitution and the division of our riches better than I do. What I do know is that, since time by itself gives to the order of things a natural inclination toward this inequality and a successive progress in it up to its last limit, it is a great imprudence to accelerate it even more by establishments which promote it. The great Sully, who loved us, would certainly have been able to tell us: theatres and drama in any little republic, and especially in Geneva, weaken the state.

If the establishment of the theatre is in itself so harmful to us, what fruit will we cull from the plays which are performed in it? The very advantages which they might procure for the peoples for whom they were composed will turn to our prejudice, in giving us for instruction what was given to them for censure, or, at least, in directing our tastes and our inclinations toward the things in the world which suit us the least. Tragedy will represent tyrants and heroes for us. What have we to do with them? Are we made to have them or to become ones ourselves? It will give us a vain admiration for power and greatness. To what end will it serve us? Will we be greater or more powerful for it? Of what import is it for us to go and study the duties of kings on the stage while neglecting to fulfil our own? Will the sterile admiration for the virtues of the theatre compensate us for the simple and modest virtues which make the good citizen? Instead of curing us of our own ridiculousness, the comedy will bring us that of others; it will persuade us that we are wrong to despise vices that are so much esteemed elsewhere. However foolish a marquess may be, he is still a marquess. Imagine what a resonance this title has in a country happy enough not to have any; and who knows how many shop drudges will think they are putting themselves in fashion by imitating the marquesses of the last century? I shall not repeat what I have already said of good faith always mocked and of the constant example of crimes made into jokes. What lessons for a people all of whose sentiments still have their natural rectitude, who believe that a rascal is always contemptible and that a good man cannot be ridiculous. What! Plato banished Homer from his republic and we will tolerate Molière in ours! What worse could happen to us than to resemble the people he depicts, even those whom he makes us like.

I have said enough, I think, about them; and I think very little better of Racine's heroes, of those heroes all gotten up, so mawkish, so tender, who, with an air of courage and virtue, provide us only with the models for the young men of whom I have spoken, given over to gallantry, softness, love, to everything which can effeminate man and mitigate his taste for his real duties. The whole French theatre breathes only tenderness; it is the great virtue to which all the others are sacrificed, or, at least, the one which is made dearest to the spectators. I do not say that this is wrong insofar as the poet's object is concerned; I know that the man without passions is a chimaera, that the appeal of the theatre is founded only on the passions, that the heart is not attracted by those which are foreign to it nor by those which we do not like to see in others although we may be subject to them ourselves. The love of humanity and of one's country are the sentiments the depiction of which most touches those who are imbued with them, but when these two passions are extinguished, there remains only love, properly so called, to take their place, because its charm is more natural and is more difficult to erase from the heart than that of all the others. However, it is not equally suitable to all men; it is rather as a supplement to good sentiments than as a good sentiment itself that it can be admitted; not that it is not laudable in itself, like every well-regulated passion, but because its excesses are dangerous and inevitable.

The most vicious of men is he who isolates himself the most, who most concentrates his heart in himself; the best is he who shares his affections equally with all his kind. It is much better to love a mistress than to love oneself alone in all the world. But whoever tenderly loves his parents, his friends, his country and humankind, degrades himself by a dissolute attachment which soon does damage to all the others and is without fail preferred to them.

On this principle, I say that there are countries where the morals [manners] are so bad that they would be only too happy to be able to raise themselves back up to the level of love; and there are others where it would be unfortunate to descend to it, and I dare to think mine is in the latter case. I will add that to·show us objects which deeply involve the passions is more dangerous than to anyone else because we have naturally only too much of a penchant to like them. Under a phlegmatic and cold manner the Genevans hide an ardent and sensitive soul easier to move than to control. In this abode of reason, beauty is not foreign nor without empire; the leaven of melancholy often causes love to ferment there; the men are only too capable of feeling violent passions, the women of inspiring them; and the sad effects that they have sometimes produced show how great is the danger of exciting them by touching and tender dramas. If the heroes of some plays subject love to duty, in admiring their force, the heart lends itself to their weakness; less is learned in giving oneself to their courage than in putting oneself in the position of having need for it. It is more exercise for virtue; but he who dares to expose his virtue to these combats deserves to succumb in them. Love, love itself, takes on the mask of virtue in order to surprise it; love clothes itself with the enthusiasm of virtue; it usurps its force; it affects its language, and, when the error is perceived, it is far too late to recover! How many men of talent, seduced by these appearances, from the tender and generous lovers that they were at first, have become by degrees vile corruptors without morals [manners], without respect for conjugal faith, without consideration for the rights of confidence and of friendship! Happy is he who is able to realize that he is on the brink of a precipice and to prevent himself from falling in! Is it in the midst of a rapid descent that one can hope to stop oneself? Is it in being moved to tenderness every day that the surmounting of tenderness can be learned? A weak penchant can easily be triumphed over; but he who knew true love and was able to vanquish it, oh! let us pardon this mortal, if he exists, for daring to pretend to virtue!

Thus, in whatever way things are envisaged, the same truth strikes us always. All that in the theatrical plays might be useful for those for whom they were written, will become detrimental for us, including even the taste which we will think we have acquired from them, which will only be a false taste without tact and delicacy, unseasonably substituted for the solidity of reason. Taste is connected with many things; the refined forms of imitation to be seen in the theatre, the comparisons to which they give occasion, reflections on the art of pleasing the spectators can cause it to germinate but do not suffice for its development. There is need of big cities, fine arts and luxury, an intimate commerce among the citizens, a strict dependence of them on one another, gallantry and even debauch, vices which one is forced to embellish; there is need, I say, of all this to cause a search for agreeable forms in everything and success in finding them. Some of these things will always be lacking to us, and we ought to tremble at acquiring the others.

We will have actors, but of what sort? Will a good troop come right off to establish itself in a city of twenty-four thousand souls? We will, then, at first have bad actors, and we will at first be bad judges. Will they form us or will we form them? We will have good plays; but, taking them for such on somebody else's word, we will be exempted from having to examine them and will gain no more in seeing them played than in reading them. For all that, we will no less play the connoisseurs and arbiters of the theatre; we will no less want to decide for our money and will be only the more ridiculous for it. It is not ridiculous to lack taste when one despises it; but it is ridiculous to pride oneself on it and only have bad taste. And, after all, what is this taste that is so much vaunted? The art of being knowing about petty things. In truth, when taste is good enough to preserve only liberty, all the rest is quite childish.

I see only one remedy for so many disadvantages; it is, in order to make the dramas of our theatre suitable to us, to compose them ourselves; we should have authors before we have actors. For it is not good that we be shown all sorts of imitations, but only those of things that are decent and befitting free men.* It is certain that plays drawn, like those of the Greeks, from the past misfortunes of the country or the present failings of the people could offer useful lessons to the spectators. Who then will be the heroes of our tragedies? Bertheliers? Lévrerys? Ah, worthy citizens, you were, doubtless, heroes but your obscurity abases you, your common names dishonor your great souls,** and we are no longer great enough ourselves to be able to admire you. Who will be our tyrants? Gentlemen of the Spoon†, bishops of Geneva, the counts of Savoy, the ancestors of a house with which we have just treated and to which we owe respect? Fifty years ago I could not have

---

* *Si quis ergo in nostram urbem venerit, qui animi sapientia in omnes possit sese vertere formas, et omnia imitari, volueritque poemata sua osten-tare, venerabimur quidem ipsum, ut sacrum, admirabilem, et jucundum: dicemus autem non esse eiusmodi hominem in republica nostra, neque fas esse ut insit; mittemusque in aliam urbem, unguento caput eius perungentes, lanaque coronantes. Nos autem austeriori minusque jucundo utemur Poeta, fabularumque fictore, utilitatis gratia, qui decori nobis rationem exprimat, et quae dici debent dicat in his formulis quas a principio pro legibus tulimus, quando cives erudire agressi sumus.* (Plat. de. Republ. lib. III.) [82]

** Philibert Berthelier was the Cato of our country, with the difference that public liberty ended with the latter and began with the former. He was holding a tame weasel when he was arrested; he handed over his sword with that pride which sits so well with unfortunate virtue; then he continued to play with his weasel without deigning to answer to the insults of his guards. He died as a martyr of liberty ought to die.

Jean Lévrery was Berthelier's Favonius, not in childishly imitating his speeches and his ways, but in dying voluntarily as he did, knowing that the example of his death would be more useful to his country than his life. Before going to the scaffold he wrote this epitaph, which had been made for his predecessor, on the wall of his prison:

> *Quid mihi mors nocuit? Virtus post fata virescit;*
> *Nec cruce, nec soevi gladio perit illa Tyranni.* [83]

† This was a brotherhood of gentlemen from Savoy who had made a vow of brigandage against the city of Geneva and who, as the mark of their association, wore a spoon hung around their necks.

answered that the Devil* and the Antichrist would not also have had their roles. With the Greeks, a people otherwise quite jocular, everything was grave and serious as soon as their country was involved; but, in this witty age when nothing escapes ridicule besides power, one dares to speak of heroism only in big states although it is only to be found in small ones.

As to comedy, it ought not to be dreamed of for us. It would cause the most frightful disorders among us; it would serve as an instrument for factions, parties, and private vengeances. Our city is so small that the most general depictions of morals [manners] would soon degenerate into satires and representations of persons. The example of ancient Athens, a city incomparably more populous than Geneva, presents us with a striking lesson; it was in the theatre that the exile of many great men and the death of Socrates was prepared for; it was by the violence of the theatre that Athens was lost, and its disasters justified only too well the chagrin to which Solon gave witness at the first performances of Thespis. What is quite certain for us is that it will be an ill omen for the republic when we see the citizens, disguised as wits, setting themselves to composing French verses and theatrical plays, talents which are not ours and which we will never possess. But let M. de Voltaire deign to compose tragedies for us on the model of *la Mort de César* and the first act of *Brutus;* and, if we must absolutely have

---

* I read, when I was young, a tragedy, which was part of the Escalade,[84] in which the Devil was actually one of the actors. I have been told that when this play was once performed, this character, as he came on stage, appeared double, as if the original had been jealous that they had had the audacity to imitate him, and instantly everybody, seized by fright, took flight, thus ending the performance. This tale is burlesque and will appear much more so in Paris than in Geneva; however, whatever suppositions we may indulge in, in this double apparition will be found a theatrical effect and a really terrifying one. I can imagine only one sight simpler and more terrible yet, that is the hand emerging from the wall and writing unknown words at the feast of Balthazar.[85] The very idea makes one shudder. It seems to me that our lyric poets are far from these sublime inventions; to no avail they make a great fuss with scenery for the purpose of horrifying. Even on the stage, not everything should be said to the eyes, but the imagination must also be excited.

a theatre, let him engage himself always to fill it with his genius
and to live as long as his plays.

I would be of the opinion that all of these reflections should be
weighed maturely before taking into consideration the taste for
adornment and dissipation which the example of the actors must
produce in our youth; but finally this example will have its effect
too, and if, in general, the laws are everywhere insufficient to repress the vices which arise out of the nature of things, as I believe
I have shown, how much more will they be so in our city where
the first sign of their weakness will be the establishment of the
actors? For it will not be, strictly speaking, they who will have
introduced this taste for dissipation; on the contrary, this taste will
have preceded them, will have introduced them, and they will only
fortify a penchant already all formed which, having caused them
to be admitted, will so much the more cause them to be maintained
with their faults.

I base myself throughout on the supposition that they will
subsist comfortably in such a little city. And I say that, if we honor
them as you claim we will, in a country where all are pretty nearly
equal, they will be the equals of everybody, and will have in addition the public favor which naturally belongs to them. They will
not, as elsewhere, be kept respectful by the great whose benevo-
lence they cultivate and the loss of whose grace they fear. The
magistrates will command their respect; granted. But these magistrates will have been private men; they might have been friendly
with the actors; they will have children who will still be friendly
with them, and wives who love pleasure. All these connections will
be means of indulgence and protection which it will be impossible
always to resist. Soon the actors, sure of impunity, will procure it
also for their imitators; it is with them that disorder will have begun, but one cannot see where it can be ended. The women, the
young, the rich, the idle, all will be for them, everything will
help them evade the laws which get in their way, everything will
promote their licence; each, in seeking to satisfy them, will think

he is working for his own pleasures. What man will dare to oppose this torrent if it is not perhaps some rigid old pastor who will not be listened to and whose sense and gravity will pass for pedantry with a thoughtless youth? Finally, if they join a bit of art and intrigue to their success, I do not give the state thirty years before they are its arbiters.* The candidates for office will be seen intriguing for their favor in order to obtain suffrages; the elections will take place in the actresses' dressing rooms, and the leaders of a free people will be the creatures of a band of histrions. The pen falls from my hand at the thought. Let the risk be dismissed as much as one pleases. Let me be accused of exaggerating the danger I foresee; I have only one word more to say. Whatever may happen, these people must reform their morals [manners] during their stay with us, or they must corrupt ours. When this alternative has ceased to alarm us, the actors can come; they can do us no more harm.

XI

THESE, Sir, are the considerations which I had to propose to the public and to you on the question which you were pleased to debate in an article to which it was, in my opinion, entirely alien. If my reasons, less strong than they seem to me, should not have sufficient weight to counterbalance yours, you will at least grant that, in a state as small as the republic of Geneva, all innovations are dangerous and that they ought never to be made without urgent and grave motives. Let the pressing necessity of this one then be shown. Where are the disorders which force us to fall back on so suspect an expedient? Is everything lost without this? Is our city so big, have vice and idleness already made such progress that it can henceforth no longer subsist without the theatre? You tell

* It must always be remembered that, in order for the drama to support itself at Geneva, this taste must become a rage; if it were only moderate, the drama would have to fail. Reason insists then that, in examining the effects of the theatre, they be measured in relation to a cause capable of supporting it.

us that it tolerates worse entertainments which shock both taste and morals [manners] alike, but there is quite a difference between presenting bad morals [manners] and attacking good ones; for this latter effect depends less on the qualities of the entertainment than on the impression it makes. In this sense, what relation is there between a few migratory farces and a resident drama, between the smutty talk of a charlatan and the regular performances of dramatic works, between the booths at the fair, built to divert the populace, and an esteemed theatre where the decent folk will think they are being instructed? One of these amusements is without consequence and stays forgotten the day after; but the other is an important affair which merits all the attention of the government. In every land it is permitted to amuse the children, and anyone who wants to can be a child without much difficulty. If these insipid shows lack taste, so much the better; they will become tiresome more quickly; if they are coarse they will be less seductive. Vice hardly insinuates itself by shocking decency but by taking on its likeness; and dirty words are more opposed to politeness than to good morals [manners]. This is why the expressions are always more refined and the ears more scrupulous in the most corrupted countries. Is it noticeable that conversations in the marketplace excite the passions of the young very much? The discrete talk of the theatre does it quite well though, and it is better that a maiden see a hundred parades than a single performance of the *Oracle*.[86]

Besides, I admit that I would, so far as I am concerned, prefer it if we could do entirely without these booths, and if, both as children and grown-ups, we were able to draw our pleasures and our duties from our state and from ourselves; but, from the fact that we ought to drive out the mountebanks, it does not follow that we must call upon the actors. You have seen the city of Marseilles in your own country fighting off a similar innovation for a long time, resisting even the reiterated orders of the minister and preserving still, in this contempt for a frivolous amusement, an honorable likeness of its ancient liberty. What an example for a city that has not yet lost its liberty.

Above all, let no one think that such an establishment can be made in the form of a trial to be abolished when harmful consequences are perceived; for those consequences are not done away with along with the theatre which produces them; they remain when their cause is removed, and, as soon as they begin to be felt, they are irremediable. Our altered morals [manners], our changed tastes, will not recover their health since they will be corrupted; even our pleasures, our innocent pleasures, will have lost their charm; the theatre will have deprived us of our taste for them forever. Idleness, become a necessity, the emptiness of our time, that we will no longer be able to fill up, will make us a burden to ourselves; the actors in parting will leave us boredom as earnest for their return; it will force us to recall them soon or to do worse. We will have done wrong in establishing the drama, we will do wrong in letting it subsist, we will do wrong in destroying it; after the first fault, we will have the choice only of our ills.

What! Ought there to be no entertainments in a republic? On the contrary, there ought to be many. It is in republics that they were born, it is in their bosom that they are seen to flourish with a truly festive air. To what peoples is it more fitting to assemble often and form among themselves sweet bonds of pleasure and joy than to those who have so many reasons to like one another and remain forever united? We already have many of these public festivals; let us have even more; I will be only the more charmed for it. But let us not adopt these exclusive entertainments which close up a small number of people in melancholy fashion in a gloomy cavern, which keep them fearful and immobile in silence and inaction, which give them only prisons, lances, soldiers, and afflicting images of servitude and inequality to see. No, happy peoples, these are not your festivals. It is in the open air, under the sky, that you ought to gather and give yourselves to the sweet sentiment of your happiness. Let your pleasures not be effeminate or mercenary;

let nothing that has an odor of constraint and selfishness poison them; let them be free and generous like you are, let the sun illuminate your innocent entertainments; you will constitute one yourselves, the worthiest it can illuminate.

But what then will be the objects of these entertainments? What will be shown in them? Nothing, if you please. With liberty, wherever abundance reigns, well-being also reigns. Plant a stake crowned with flowers in the middle of a square; gather the people together there, and you will have a festival. Do better yet; let the spectators become an entertainment to themselves; make them actors themselves; do it so that each sees and loves himself in the others so that all will be better united. I need not have recourse to the games of the ancient Greeks; there are modern ones which are still in existence, and I find them precisely in our city. Every year we have reviews, public prizes, kings of the harquebus, the cannon, and sailing. Institutions so useful* and so agreeable cannot be too much multiplied; of such kings there cannot be too many. Why

* It does not suffice that the people have bread and live in their stations. They must live in them pleasantly, in order that they fulfil their duties better, that they torment themselves less over changing their stations, that public order be better established. Good morals [manners] depend more than is thought on each man's being satisfied in his estate. Deceit and the spirit of intrigue come from uneasiness and discontentment; everything goes badly when one aspires to the position of another. One must like his trade to do it well. The disposition of the state is only good and solid when, each feeling in his place, the private forces are united and co-operate for the public good instead of wasting themselves one against the other as they do in every badly constituted state. This given, what must we think of those who would wish to take the festivals, the pleasures, and every form of amusement away from the people as so many distractions which turn them away from their work? This maxim is barbarous and false. Too bad, if the people have only the time to earn their bread; they must still have some in which to eat it with joy; otherwise they will not earn it for long. This just and beneficent God, who wants them to keep busy, wants also that they relax; nature imposes exercises and repose, pleasure and pain alike upon them. The distaste for labor overwhelms the unfortunate more than labor itself. Do you then want to make a people active and laborious? Give them festivals, offer them amusements which make them like their stations and prevent them from craving for a sweeter one. Days thus lost will turn the others to better account. Preside at their pleasures in order to make them decent; this is the true means to animate their labors.

should we not do to make ourselves active and robust what we do to become skilled in the use of arms? Has the republic less need of workers than of soldiers? Why should we not found, on the model of the military prizes, other prizes for gymnastics, wrestling, runnings, discus, and the various bodily exercises? Why should we not animate our boatmen by contests on the lake? Could there be an entertainment in the world more brilliant than seeing, on this vast and superb body of water, hundreds of boats, elegantly equipped, starting together at the given signal to go and capture a flag planted at the finish, then serving as a cortege for the victor returning in triumph to receive his well-earned prize? All festivals of this sort are expensive only insofar as one wishes them to be, and the gathering alone renders them quite magnificent. Nevertheless, one must have been there with the Genevans to understand with what ardor they devote themselves to them. They are unrecognizable; they are no longer that steady people which never deviates from its economic rules; they are no longer those slow reasoners who weigh everything, including joking, in the scale of judgment. The people are lively, gay, and tender; their hearts are then in their eyes as they are always on their lips; they seek to communicate their joy and their pleasures. They invite, importune, and coerce the new arrivals and dispute over them. All the societies constitute but one, all become common to all. It is almost a matter of indifference at which table one seats oneself. It would be the image of Lacedaemon if a certain lavishness did not prevail here; but this very lavishness is at this time in its place, and the sight of the abundance makes that of the liberty which produces it more moving.

Winter, a time consecrated to the private association of friends, is less appropriate to public festivals. There is, however, one sort concerning which I wish there were not so many scrupulous doubts raised, that is, the balls for young marriageable persons. I have never understood why people are so worried about dancing and the gatherings it occasions, as if there were something worse about dancing than singing, as if these amusements were not both equally an inspiration of nature, as if it were a crime for those who are destined to be united to be merry together in a decent recreation. Man and woman were formed for one another. God wants them to fulfil their destiny, and certainly the first and holiest of all the bonds of society is marriage. All the false religions combat nature; ours alone, which follows and regulates it, proclaims a divine institution and one suitable for man. It ought not to add to the impediments which the civil order provides to marriage, difficulties which the Gospel does not prescribe and that every good government condemns. But let me be instructed as to where young marriageable persons will have occasion to get a taste for one another and to see one another with more propriety and circumspection than in a gathering where the eyes of the public are constantly open and upon them, forcing them to be reserved, modest, and to watch themselves most carefully? In what way is God offended by an agreeable exercise, one that is salutary and befitting the vivacity of young people, which consists in presenting themselves to one another with grace and seemliness, and on which the spectator imposes a gravity out of which they would not dare to step for an instant? Can a more decent way of not deceiving one another, at least as to their persons, be imagined, or one which better permits them to show themselves off, with the charms and the faults which they might possess, to the people whose interest it is to know them well before being obliged to love them? Does not the duty of cherishing each other reciprocally imply that of pleasing each other; and is it not an attention worthy of two virtuous and Christian persons who seek to be united to prepare their hearts in this way for the mutual love which God imposes on them?

What happens in those places where an eternal constraint prevails, where the most innocent gaiety is punished as a crime, where the young people of the two sexes never dare to gather in public, and where the indiscreet severity of a pastor can only preach a servile uneasiness, dreariness, and boredom in the name of God? They evade intolerable tyranny, which nature and reason disavow.

For the permitted pleasures which a lively and frolicsome youth is denied are substituted more dangerous ones. Private meetings adroitly concerted take the place of public gatherings. By dint of hiding themselves as if they were guilty, they are tempted to become so. Innocent joy is likely to evaporate in the full light of day; but vice is a friend of shadows, and never have innocence and mystery lived long together.

As for me, far from blaming such simple entertainments, I wish they were publicly authorized and that all private disorder were anticipated by converting them into solemn and periodic balls, open without distinction to all the marriageable young. I wish that a magistrate,* named by the council, would not think it beneath him to preside at these balls. I wish that the fathers and mothers would attend to watch over their children, as witnesses of their grace and their address, of the applause they may have merited, and thus to enjoy the sweetest entertainment [*spectacle*] that can move a paternal heart. I wish that in general all married women be admitted among the number of the spectators and judges without being permitted to profane conjugal dignity by dancing themselves; for, to what decent purpose could they thus show themselves off in public? I wish that in the hall there be formed a comfortable and honorable section reserved for the old people of both sexes who, having already given citizens to the country, would now see their grandchildren prepare themselves to become citizens. I wish that no one enter or leave without saluting this box, and that all the young couples come before beginning and after having finished their dance and make a deep bow there in order to accustom them early to respect old age. I do not doubt

* Over every guild and public society of which our state is composed presides one of these magistrates under the name of *Lord-Commissioner*. They attend all the gatherings and even the feasts. Their presence does not prevent a decent familiarity among the members of the association; but it maintains everyone in the respect that they ought to have for the laws, morals [manners], and propriety, even in the midst of joy and pleasure. This institution is very fine and forms one of the great bonds which unite the people to their leaders.

that this pleasant meeting of the two extremes of human life will give to this gathering a certain touching aspect and that sometimes in this box tears will be seen being shed, tears of joy and memory, capable perhaps of eliciting them from a sensitive spectator. I wish that every year, at the last ball, the young girl, who during the preceding one has comported herself most decently, most modestly, and has most pleased everyone in the judgment of the members of the box, be honored with a crown from the hand of the Lord Commissioner* and with the title of Queen of the Ball, which she will bear throughout the year. I wish that at the close of this gathering she be brought back home by a cortege, and that her father and mother be congratulated and thanked for having a daughter of so good a nature and for raising her so well. Finally, I wish that, if she happens to marry in the course of the year, the magistrates make her a present or accord her some public distinction so that this honor be a thing serious enough never to become a subject of joking.

It is true that often a bit of partiality might be feared if the age of the judges did not leave all preference to merit. And even if modest beauty were sometimes favored, what would be the great harm in that? Having more assaults to sustain, does it not need to be encouraged more? Is it not a gift of nature just as talents are? What harm is there if beauty obtains some honors which excite it to make itself worthy of them and can content vanity without offending virtue?

In perfecting this project along these lines and giving a tone of gallantry and amusement to it, these festivals would serve many useful purposes which would make of them an important component of the training in law and order and good morals [manners]. The young, having certain and decent meeting places, would be less tempted to seek for more dangerous ones. Each sex would devote itself more patiently in the intervals to occupations and pleasures which are fitting to it, and would be more easily consoled for being deprived of the continual company of the other. Indi-

* See the preceding note.

viduals in every station, especially fathers and mothers, would have the resource of an agreeable entertainment. The attentions to the adornment of their daughters would be an object of amusement for the women which in its turn would provide diversion for many others. And this adornment, having an innocent and laudable object, would there be entirely in its place. These occasions for gathering in order to form unions and for arranging the establishment of families would be frequent means for reconciling divided families and bolstering the peace so necessary in our state. Without altering the authority of fathers, the inclinations of children would be somewhat freer; the first choice would depend somewhat more on their hearts; the agreements of age, temperament, taste, and character would be consulted somewhat more; and less attention would be paid to those of station and fortune which make bad matches when they are satisfied at the expense of the others. The relations becoming easier, the marriages would be more frequent; these marriages, less circumscribed by rank, would prevent the emergence of parties, temper excessive inequality, and maintain the body of the people better in the spirit of its constitution; these balls, thus directed, would bring the people together not so much for a public entertainment as for the gathering of a big family, and from the bosom of joy and pleasures would be born the preservation, the concord, and the prosperity of the republic.*

* It is sometimes amusing for me to imagine the judgments that many will make of my tastes on the basis of my writings. On the basis of this one they will not fail to say: "that man is crazy about dancing"; it bores me to watch dancing; "he cannot bear the drama"; I love the drama passionately; "he has an aversion to women"; on that score I shall be only too easily vindicated: "he is vexed at actors"; I have every reason to be pleased with them, and friendship with the only one of them whom I have known personally can only do honor to a decent man. Same judgment on the poets whose plays I am forced to censure: those who are dead will not be to my taste, and I will be piqued with the living. The truth is that Racine charms me and that I have never willingly missed a performance of Molière. If I have spoken less of Corneille, it is because, having less frequented his plays and lacking books, I do not remember him well enough to cite him. As to the author of *Atrée* and *Catalina*, I have seen him only once, and this was to receive a service from him. I esteem his genius and respect his old age; but, whatever honor I have for his

On the basis of these ideas it would be easy to establish, at small cost and without danger, more entertainments than are necessary to make a visit to our city pleasant and cheerful, even for foreigners who, finding nothing like it anywhere else, would come at least to see something unique. Although, to tell the truth, for many good reasons I regard this influx as a problem far more than as an advantage; and I am persuaded, as for myself, that never did a foreigner come to Geneva who did not do more harm than good.

But do you know, Sir, whom we ought to try to attract and keep within our walls? The Genevans themselves who, with a sincere love of their country, all have so great an inclination to travel that there is no land where they are not to be found dispersed. Half of our citizens, scattered throughout the rest of Europe and the world, live and die far from their country; I would cite myself with more sorrow if I were less useless to it. I know that we are forced to go abroad and seek the resources which our soil refuses to us, and that we could hardly subsist if we were confined there; but at least let this banishment not be eternal for all. Let those whose labors Heaven has blest come, like the bee, bringing the fruit back to the hive; let them gladden their fellow citizens with

---

person, I owe only justice to his plays, and I cannot acquit my debts at the expense of the public good and the truth. If my writings inspire me with some pride, it is for the purity of intention which dictates them, it is for the disinterestedness for which few authors have given me the example and which very few will wish to imitate. Never did personal views soil the desire to be useful to others which put the pen in my hand and I have almost always written against my own interest. *Vitam impendere vero:*[87] this is the motto I have chosen and of which I feel I am worthy. Readers, I may deceive myself, but I do not deceive you willingly; beware of my errors and not my bad faith. Love of the public good is the only passion which causes me to speak to the public; I can then forget myself, and if someone offends me, I keep quiet about him for fear that anger make me unjust. This maxim is beneficial for my enemies in that they can hurt me at their leisure and without fear of reprisals, for the readers who do not fear that my hate imposes on them, and especially for me who, keeping quiet while I am insulted, suffer at least only the hurt which is done me and not that which I would experience in returning it. Holy and pure truth to whom I have consecrated my life, never will my passions soil the sincere love which I have for thee; neither interest nor fear can corrupt the homage that I am wont to offer to thee, and my pen will refuse thee only what it fears to accord to vengeance.

the sight of their fortune, animate the emulation of the young, enrich their country with their wealth, and enjoy modestly at home a substance decently acquired abroad. Is it with theatres, always less perfect in our city than elsewhere, that they will be made to return? Will they leave the theatre of Paris or London to go to see that of Geneva? No, no, Sir, it is not thus that they can be brought back. Each must feel that he could not find elsewhere what he left in his country; an invincible charm must recall him to the seat he ought never to have quitted; the memory of their first exercises, their first entertainments, their first pleasures, must remain profoundly engraved in their hearts; the sweet impressions made during youth must live and be strengthened at an advanced age while countless others are blotted out; in the midst of the pomp of great states and their dreary magnificence, a secret voice must incessantly cry out to them from the depths of their souls: Ah! where are the games and festivals of my youth? Where is the concord of the citizens? Where is the public fraternity? Where is the pure joy and the real gaiety? Where are the peace, the liberty, the equity, the innocence? Let us go and seek out all that again. My God! with the heart of a Genevan, with a city so cheerful, a land so charming, a government so just, pleasures so true and so pure and all that is needed to delight in them, what can prevent us all from adoring our country?

Thus did that Sparta, which I shall have never cited enough as the example that we ought to follow, recall its citizens by modest festivals and games without pomp; thus in Athens, in the midst of the fine arts, thus in Susa, in the lap of luxury and softness, the bored Spartan longed for his coarse feasts and his fatiguing exercises. It is at Sparta that, in laborious idleness, everything was pleasure and entertainment; it is there that the harshest labors passed for recreations and that small relaxations formed a public instruction; it is there that the citizens, constantly assembled, consecrated the whole of life to amusements which were the great business of the state and to games from which they relaxed only for war.

I already hear the wits asking me if, among so many marvelous instructions, I do not also want to introduce the dances of the young Lacedaemonian girls into the Genevan festivals? I answer that I should like to believe that our eyes and our hearts were chaste enough to bear such a sight, and that young people in this state at Geneva, as at Sparta, would be clothed by public decency. But, whatever esteem I have for my fellow citizens, I know too well how far it is from them to the Lacedaemonians; and I propose for them only the Spartan institutions of which they are not yet incapable. If the wise Plutarch took it upon himself to justify the practice in question, why must I take it upon myself after him?[88] Everything is said in admitting that this practice was fitting only for the pupils of Lycurgus, that their frugal and laborious lives, their pure and severe morals [manners], the strength of soul which belonged to them, could alone make innocent for their eyes an entertainment so shocking for any people which is only decent.

But can it be thought that the artful dress of our women is fundamentally less dangerous than an absolute nudity the habit of which would soon turn the first effects into indifference and perhaps distaste? Is it not known that statues and paintings only offend the eyes when a mixture of clothing renders the nudity obscene? The immediate power of the senses is weak and limited; it is through the intermediary of the imagination that they make their greatest ravages; it is the business of the imagination to irritate the desires in lending to their objects even more attractions than nature gave them; it is the imagination which scandalizes the eye in revealing to it what it sees not only as naked but as something that ought to be clothed. There is no garment so modest that a glance inflamed by imagination does not penetrate with its desires. A young Chinese woman extending the tip of her foot, covered and shod, will wreak more havoc in Peking than the most beautiful girl in the world dancing stark naked on the banks of the Taygetus. But when they dress with so much art and so little correctness as the modern women do, when less is shown only to make more desired, when the obstacle set before the eyes serves only to excite the imagina-

tion more, when a part of the object is hidden only to set off what
is exposed:

Heu! male tum mites defendit pampinus uvas [89]

Let us finish these many digressions. Thank Heaven, this is the
last; I am at the end of this writing. I presented the festivals of Lacedaemon as a model for those I should like to see among us. It is not
only because of their object but also their simplicity that I find them
worthy of recommendation; without pomp, without luxury, without display, everything in them breathes, along with a secret patri-
otic charm which makes them attractive, a certain martial spirit
befitting free men.* Without business and without pleasures, at

* I remember having been struck in my childhood by a rather simple
entertainment, the impression of which has nevertheless always stayed with
me in spite of time and variety of experience. The regiment of Saint-Gervais
had done its exercises, and, according to the custom, they had supped by
companies; most of those who formed them gathered after supper in the St.
Gervais square and started dancing all together, officers and soldiers, around
the fountain, to the basin of which the drummers, the fifers and the torch
bearers had mounted. A dance of men, cheered by a long meal, would seem
to present nothing very interesting to see; however, the harmony of five or
six hundred men in uniform, holding one another by the hand and forming
a long ribbon which wound around, serpent-like, in cadence and without
confusion, with countless turns and returns, countless sorts of figured evolu-
tions, the excellence of the tunes which animated them, the sound of the
drums, the glare of the torches, a certain military pomp in the midst of
pleasure, all this created a very lively sensation that could not be experienced
coldly. It was late; the women were in bed; all of them got up. Soon the windows were full of female spectators who gave a new zeal to the actors; they
could not long confine themselves to their windows and they came down;
the wives came to their husbands, the servants brought wine; even the children, awakened by the noise, ran half-clothed amidst their fathers and
mothers. The dance was suspended; now there were only embraces, laughs,
healths, and caresses. There resulted from all this a general emotion that I
could not describe but which, in universal gaiety, is quite naturally felt in the
midst of all that is dear to us. My father, embracing me, was seized with
trembling which I think I still feel and share. "Jean-Jacques," he said to me,
"love your country. Do you see these good Genevans? They are all friends,
they are all brothers; joy and concord reign in their midst. You are a Genevan;
one day you will see other peoples; but even if you should travel as much as
your father, you will not find their likes."

They wanted to pick up the dance again, but it was impossible; they did
not know what they were doing any more; all heads were spinning with a

least those that bear the name with us, in this sweet uniformity they spent the day without finding it too long, and life without finding it too short. They came back every evening, cheerful and hearty, took their frugal meal, content with their country, their fellow citizens, and themselves. If some example of their public pastimes be asked for, here is one reported by Plutarch.[90] There were, he says, always three dances in as many bands, divided according to the differences in age; and they danced to the singing of each band. That of the old began first, singing the following couplet:

> We were once young,
> Valiant and hardy

There followed that of the men who sang in their turn, beating their arms in cadence:

> We are so now
> ready for all comers

and then came the children, who answered them singing with all their force:

> And we will soon be so,
> we who will surpass you all.

These, Sir, are the entertainments which republics need. As to the one your article *Geneva* forced me to treat in this essay, if ever private interest succeeds in establishing it within our walls, I predict unhappy effects; I have shown some of them, I could show more; but that would be to fear too much an imaginary misfortune which the vigilance of our magistrates will be able to prevent. I do

drunkenness sweeter than that of wine. After staying somewhat longer to laugh and chat in the square, they had to part, each withdrawing peaceably with his family; and this is how these lovable and prudent women brought their husbands back home, not in disturbing their pleasures but in going to share them. I am well aware that this entertainment, which moved me so, would be without appeal for countless others; one must have eyes made for seeing it and a heart made for feeling it. No, the only pure joy is public joy, and the true sentiments of nature reign only over the people. Ah! Dignity, daughter of pride and mother of boredom, have your melancholy slaves ever had a similar moment in their lives?

not pretend to instruct men wiser than me. It suffices for me to have said enough to console the youth of my land for being deprived of an amusement which would cost the country so dear. I exhort this fortunate youth to profit from the opinion with which your article ends.[91] May it recognize and merit its fate! May it always feel how much solid happiness is preferable to the vain pleasures which destroy it! May it transmit to its descendants the virtues, the liberty, and the peace which it has inherited from its fathers! This is the last wish with which I end my writings; it is the one with which my life will end.

Appendix

The Article "Geneva"
by d'Alembert[*]

The city of Geneva is situated on two hills at the end of the lake which today bears its name but which was formerly called Lake Leman. The site is most agreeable; on one side the lake is to be seen, on the other, the Rhone; in the surroundings, a smiling countryside; along the lake, slopes covered with country houses; and a few leagues away, the ever snowy peaks of the Alps, which seem to be mountains of silver when the sun shines on them on fair days. The port of Geneva on the lake, with its jetties, boats, and markets, and its position between France, Italy, and Germany, make it rich, commercial, and full of skills and industry. There are many fine buildings and agreeable walks; the streets are lighted at night, and they have constructed a very simple pumping machine on the Rhone which supplies water up to the highest sections, at an elevation of one hundred feet. The lake is about eighteen leagues long and four to five in breadth at its widest. It is a sort of little sea which has its tempests and which produces other singular phenomena.

Julius Caesar speaks about Geneva as a city of the Allobroges, then a Roman province; he went there to combat the crossing of the Helvetians, who have since been named the Swiss. When Christianity was introduced into this city, it became an episcopal seat, a suffragan of Vienna. At the beginning of the fifth century the emperor Honorius ceded it to the Burgundians, who were ousted in 534 by the Frankish kings. When Charlemagne, toward the end of the ninth century, went to fight the kings of the Lombards and deliver the pope, who handsomely rewarded him for it with the imperial crown, that prince stopped at Geneva and made it the meeting place for his army. The

[*] *Encyclopédie*, VII, 578.

city was afterwards annexed by inheritance to the German empire, and Conrad went there to take the imperial crown in 1034. But, since the emperors who succeeded him were occupied for three hundred years with the very important troubles which the popes stirred up for them and had neglected to keep an eye on Geneva, it gradually shook off the yoke and became an imperial city which had its bishop for prince or, rather, for lord; for the authority of the bishop was tempered by that of the citizens. The coat of arms which it took at this time expressed this mixed constitution; there was on one side an imperial eagle and on the other a key representing the power of the Church, with this motto, *Post tenebras lux*. The city of Geneva kept its arms after having renounced the Roman Church; they have nothing more in common with the papacy than the key they have in their escutcheon; it is even rather surprising that they should have kept them after having, as it were, superstitiously broken all the ties they had with Rome. They apparently thought that the motto, *Post tenebras lux*, which expresses perfectly, so they believe, their present state in regard to religion, permitted them to change nothing in their coat of arms.

The dukes of Savoy, neighbors of Geneva sometimes supported by the bishops, tried on different occasions to establish their authority gradually in this city; but it resisted courageously, sustained by the alliance of Freiburg and Bern. It was then, that is to say around 1526, that the Council of the Two Hundred was established. The opinions of Luther and Zwingli began to be introduced; Bern had adopted them; Geneva was tasting them; it admitted them in 1535; the papacy was abolished; and the bishop, who still assumes the title of Bishop of Geneva without having any more jurisdiction there than the bishop of Babylon has in his diocese, resides at Annecy since that time.

A Latin inscription in memory of the abolition of the Catholic religion is still to be seen between the two doors of the Geneva town hall. The pope is called the Antichrist in it; this expression, in which the fanaticism of liberty and novelty indulged itself during a still semibarbaric age, seems to us hardly worthy today of a city so philosophic. We dare to request it to substitute for this insulting and crude memorial a truer, nobler, and simpler inscription. For the Catholics, the pope is the head of the true Church; for the wise and moderate Protestants, he is a sovereign whom they respect as a prince without obeying him; but in an age such as ours, he is no longer the Antichrist for anyone.

Geneva, in order to defend its liberty against the enterprises of the dukes of Savoy and its bishops, fortified itself with the alliance of Zurich and especially with that of France. It is with this aid that it resisted the arms of Charles-Emmanuel and the riches of Philip II, that prince whose ambition, despotism, cruelty, and superstition assure to his memory the execration of posterity. Henry IV, who had aided Geneva with three hundred soldiers, soon afterwards had need himself of its aid; Geneva was not useless to him at the time of the League, and on other occasions; and out of this have issued the privileges which the Genevans enjoy in France like the Swiss.

These people, wishing to make their city celebrated, called Calvin, who enjoyed with justice a great reputation, man of letters of the first order, writing in Latin as well as one can in a dead language, and in French with a singular purity for his time; that purity, which our grammarians still admire today, makes his writings quite superior to almost all those of the same age, as the works of the gentlemen of Port-Royal are still distinguished today, for the same reason, from the barbaric rhapsodies of their adversaries and contemporaries. Calvin, able jurisconsult and theologian as enlightened as a heretic can be, set up in concert with the magistrates a collection of civil and ecclesiastical laws which was approved by the people in 1543 and which has become the fundamental code of the republic. The superfluous ecclesiastical riches, which had served before the Reformation for the support of the bishops' luxury and that of their subordinates, were applied to the foundation of a poorhouse, a college, and an academy; but the wars which Geneva had to bear for nearly sixty years kept the arts and commerce as well as the sciences from flourishing there. Finally, the ill success of the scaling of the walls [*escalade*] attempted by the Duke of Savoy marked the beginning of this republic's tranquillity. The Genevans repulsed their enemies, who had attacked them by surprise; and, to give the Duke of Savoy a distaste for such enterprises, they hanged thirteen of the principal enemy generals. They thought they could treat men who had attacked their city without declaration of war like highway robbers; for this singular and new policy, which consists in making war without having declared it, was not yet known in Europe; and, although it has been practiced by the big states since then, it is too prejudicial to the little ones ever to be to their taste.

Duke Charles-Emmanuel, seeing himself repulsed and his generals hanged, gave up trying to seize Geneva. His example served as a lesson to his successors; and since that time this city has not ceased to increase its population, to enrich itself, and to adorn itself in the midst of peace. Some civil dissensions, the last of which broke out in 1738, have from time to time slightly troubled the tranquillity of the republic; but everything has been happily pacified by the mediation of France and the confederated cantons; and external security is more strongly established than ever by two new treaties, one with France in 1749, the other with the king of Sardinia in 1754.

It is a very remarkable thing that a city which numbers hardly twenty-four thousand souls and whose outlying lands do not contain thirty villages, is nevertheless a sovereign state and one of the most flourishing cities of Europe. Rich in its liberty and its commerce, it often sees everything in flames around it without ever feeling them; the events which agitate Europe are for it only a spectacle which it enjoys without taking part; attached to the French by its alliances and by its commerce, to the English by its commerce and religion, it pronounces with impartiality on the justice of the wars which these two powerful nations make against one another, although it is otherwise too prudent to take any part in these wars; it judges all the sovereigns of Europe without flattering them, without wounding them, and without fearing them.

The city is well fortified, especially on the side of that prince it fears the most, the king of Sardinia. On the side of France it is practically open and without defense. But military service is performed there as in a warlike city; the arsenals and magazines are well supplied; every citizen is a soldier there as in Switzerland and ancient Rome. The Genevans are permitted to serve in foreign armies; but the state furnishes no power with official companies and tolerates no recruitment in its territory.

Although the city is rich, the state is poor because of the repugnance that the people manifest for new taxes, even the least onerous. The revenue of the state does not attain five hundred thousand pounds in French money; but the admirable economy with which it is administered provides for everything and even produces sums in reserve for extraordinary needs.

There is a distinction among four orders of persons in Geneva: the citizens, who are the sons of townsmen and are born in the city; they alone can enter the magistracy; the townsmen, who are sons of townsmen or citizens but are born in foreign countries, or foreigners who have acquired the right to be townsmen, which the magistrates can confer; they belong to the General Council and even to the Grand Council called the Two Hundred. The inhabitants are foreigners who have permission from the magistrates to live in the city but who can do nothing else in it. Finally, the natives are sons of the inhabitants; they have some more privileges than their fathers but they are excluded from the government.

At the head of the republic are four syndics who can hold the office for only one year and cannot return to it before four years. To the syndics is joined the small council composed of twenty councillors, a treasurer, and two secretaries of state, and another body called the judicial council. The daily affairs which demand dispatch, whether criminal or civil, are the object of these two bodies.

The grand council is composed of two hundred fifty citizens or townsmen; it is the judge of the important civil cases, it grants pardons, it strikes money, it elects the members of the small council, it deliberates on what ought to be brought before the general council. This general council embraces the entire citizen body except for those who are not yet twenty-five, bankrupt individuals, and those who have had some disgrace. The legislative power belongs to this assembly as does the right of war and peace, alliance, taxation, and the election of the principal magistrates, which takes place in the cathedral with great order and propriety although the number of voters is around fifteen hundred.

It can be seen from this account that the government of Geneva has all of the advantages and none of the difficulties of democracy; everything is under the direction of the syndics, everything emanates from the small council for deliberation, and everything returns to it for execution; thus it seems as if the city of Geneva took as its model that wise law of the ancient German government: *De minoribus rebus principes consultant, de majoribus omnes; ita tamen, ut ea quorum penes plebem arbitrium est, apud principes praetractentur.* (Tacit, *De Mor. German.*)[92]

The civil law of Geneva is almost entirely drawn from Roman law, with some modifications; for example, a father can leave only half of his wealth to whom he pleases; the rest is divided equally among his children. This law assures, on the one hand, the independence of the children; on the other, it forestalls the injustice of the fathers.

M. de Montesquieu rightly calls a *fine law* the one which excludes from public office the citizens who do not discharge the debts of their fathers after their death, and, so much the more, those who do not discharge their own debts.

They do not extend the degrees of kinship which prohibit marriage beyond those designated by *Leviticus;* thus, first cousins can be married to one another; but there is also no dispensation in the prohibited cases. Divorce is accorded in cases of adultery or malicious desertion, after judicial proclamations.

Criminal justice is exercised with more exactitude than rigor. Torture, already abolished in many states, and which ought to be abolished everywhere as a useless cruelty, is proscribed in Geneva; it is applied only to criminals already condemned to death, in order to discover their accomplices if it is necessary. The defendant can demand to be informed of the charges against him and can be aided by his relatives and a lawyer in pleading his case before the judges in open session. Criminal sentences are delivered by the syndics in the public place with great formality.

No hereditary dignities are recognized in Geneva; the son of a first magistrate stays lost in the crowd if he does not distinguish himself from it by his merit. Neither nobility nor riches gives rank, prerogative, or facility in elevating oneself to office; intrigues are severely forbidden. The offices are so unremunerative that they cannot excite cupidity; they can only tempt noble souls because of the respect which attaches to them.

There are few lawsuits; most are conciliated by common friends, even by the lawyers, and by the judges.

Sumptuary laws forbid the use of jewelry and gold, limit funeral expenses, and oblige all the citizens to go on foot in the streets; there are carriages only for the country. These laws, which would be regarded in France as too severe and almost as barbarous and inhuman, are not at all destructive of the true comforts of life which can always be gotten at small cost; they only curtail ostentation, which does not contribute to happiness and which ruins men without being useful.

There is no city where there are more happy marriages; Geneva is on this point two hundred years ahead of our morals [manners]. Because of the regulations against luxury they are not afraid of having many children; thus luxury is not, as in France, one of the great obstacles to population.

[The sections on the theatre appear in Rousseau's text, pp. 4-5.]

Geneva has a university called the academy where the young are taught without payment. The professors can become magistrates and, indeed, many have done so, which does a great deal to stimulate the emulation and celebrity of the academy. Some years ago a school of drawing was established. The lawyers, the notaries, and the doctors form bodies in which one can be licensed only after public examinations; and all the handicraft guilds also have their regulations, their apprenticeships, and their masterpieces.

The public library is well stocked; it contains twenty-six thousand volumes and a rather large number of manuscripts. These books are loaned to all the citizens; thus everyone reads and is enlightened; hence, the people are better educated in Geneva than anywhere else. It has not been observed that this is an evil as it is claimed it would be in our country. Perhaps the Genevans and our statesmen are both right.

After England, Geneva was the first to accept vaccination for smallpox, vaccination which has such difficulty getting established in France but which will, nevertheless, be established there although many of our physicians still fight it, as their predecessors fought the circulation of the blood, emetics, and so many other incontestable truths or useful practices.

All the sciences and almost all the arts have been so well cultivated in Geneva that one would be astonished to see the list of the scientists and artists of all sorts that this city has produced in the last two hundred years. It has even sometimes had the advantage of possessing some celebrated foreigners who have been drawn to retire there by its agreeable situation and the liberty which is enjoyed. M. de Voltaire, who established his residence there four years ago, finds among these republicans the same marks of esteem and respect he has received from many monarchs.

The most flourishing industry at Geneva is watchmaking; it employs more than five thousand persons, that is to say, more than a fifth of the citizens. The other arts are not neglected, among them agriculture. The land's lack of fertility is compensated for by dint of care and work.

All the houses are built of stone, which very often prevents fires, which are, by the way, promptly extinguished by the excellent organization established for the purpose.

The poorhouses in Geneva are not as elsewhere, simply refuges for the sick and infirm poor; hospitality is extended to poor transients; but, more important, a number of little pensions are drawn from it which are distributed to poor families to help them to live without moving and without giving up their work. The poorhouses spend more than triple their income every year, so abundant is charity of all sorts.

The religion of Geneva remains for us to talk about. It is the part of this article which perhaps most interests philosophers. We are now going to discuss this particular; but we beg our readers to remember that we are here only historians, not controversialists. Our articles on theology are destined to serve as antidotes to this one, and to recount here is not to approve. We refer our readers, then, to the words *Eucharist, Hell, Faith, Christianity*, etc., in order to fortify them in advance against what we are going to say.

The ecclesiastical constitution of Geneva is purely presbyterian: no bishops, even fewer canons; it is not that they disapprove of the episcopate, but rather, since they do not believe in divine right, that it was thought that pastors less rich and less important than bishops were more appropriate to a little republic.

The ministers are either pastors like our curés, or postulants, like our priests without a living. The revenue of the pastors does not exceed twelve hundred pounds, without any surplice fees. The state pays them, for the Church has nothing. The ministers are accepted only when they are twenty-four, after very rigid examinations of their learning and their morals [manners], the example of which it would be desirable for most of our Catholic churches to follow.

The ecclesiastics have nothing to do at funerals; it is a purely civil act which is carried out without pomp; they believe in Geneva that it is ridiculous to be ostentatious after death. They bury in a vast cemetery rather distant from the city, a practice which should be followed elsewhere. The clergy of Geneva has exemplary morals [manners]; the ministers live in harmony; they are not seen, as in other countries, disputing with bitterness among themselves about unintelligible matters, persecuting one another mutually, indecently accusing one another before the magistrates. They are, however, far from all thinking the same on the articles which are elsewhere regarded as the most important to religion. Many do not believe any more in the divinity of Jesus Christ, of which their leader Calvin was so zealous a defender and for which he had Servet burned. When one speaks to them about this torture, which does some injustice to the charity and moderation of their patriarch, they limit themselves, if it is a Catholic speaking to them, to opposing the torture of Servet to the abominable St. Bartholomew's day which every good Frenchman desires to blot out from our history with his blood; and the torture of John Hus which the Catholics themselves, they say, no longer undertake to justify, in which humanity and good faith were equally violated, and which ought to cover the name of the Emperor Sigismund with eternal opprobrium.

"It is no small example of the progress of human reason," says M. de Voltaire, "that they could print in Geneva, with public approval (in the *Essay on Universal History* of that author) that Calvin had an odious soul as well as an enlightened mind. The murder of Servet today seems abominable." We believe that the praises owed this noble freedom to think and to write should be evenly divided among the author, his age, and Geneva. How many countries there are in which philosophy has made no less progress, but in which reason does not dare to raise its voice to strike down what it condemns in silence, in which too many pusillanimous writers, who are called prudent, respect prejudices which they could combat with as much propriety as security.

Hell, one of the principal points of our belief, is today no longer one for many of Geneva's ministers; it would, according to them, insult the Divinity to imagine that this Being, full of goodness and justice, was capable of punishing our faults by an eternity of torments. They interpret as well as they can the explicit passages which are contrary to their opinion, claiming that one must never take literally, in the holy books, everything which seems to wound humanity and reason. They believe, hence, that there are punishments in another life, but for a time; thus purgatory, which was one of the principal causes of the separation of the Protestants from the Roman Church, is today the only punishment many of them admit after death; here is a new touch to add to the history of human contradictions.

To sum up in a word, many of Geneva's pastors have no religion other than a complete Socinianism, rejecting all those things which are called mysteries, and imagining that the first principle of a true religion is to propose nothing to belief which offends reason; so that when one presses them on the *necessity* of revelation, that dogma so essential to Christianity, many substitute for it the term *utility*, which seems to them milder; in that, if they are not orthodox, they are at least consequent with their principles.

A clergy which thinks thus ought to be tolerant, and it is actually tolerant enough not to be well viewed by the ministers of the other Reformed churches. It can be said, moreover, without intending to approve of Geneva's religion otherwise, that there are few countries in which the theologians and the ecclesiastics are more hostile to superstition. And, as a result, since intolerance and superstition only serve to increase the number of disbelievers, they complain less at Geneva than elsewhere of the progress of disbelief. This is not surprising, since religion has been practically reduced to the adoration of a single God, at least among all those not of the common classes; the respect for Jesus Christ and the Scripture is perhaps the only thing which distinguishes the Christianity of Geneva from a pure deism.

The ecclesiastics do what is even better than being tolerant; they limit themselves strictly to their duties in being the first to give to the citizens the example of submission to the laws. The consistory, established to watch over morals [manners], administers only spiritual punishments. The great quarrel between the priesthood and the state, which in ages of ignorance shook the crowns of so many emperors and which, as we know only too well, causes disagreeable troubles in more enlightened ages, is not known in Geneva; the clergy does nothing without the approval of the magistrates.

Worship is very simple; no images, no candelabra, no ornaments in the churches. They have, however, just put a door in rather good taste on the cathedral; perhaps they will, little by little, come to the decoration of the interiors of the temples. What would really be wrong with having paintings and statues while warning the people, if one pleases, not to worship them and to regard them only as monuments established for the purpose of relating in a striking and agreeable way the principal events of religion? The arts would gain by it without superstition's profiting. We speak here in terms of the principles of the Genevan pastors and not in terms of those of the Catholic Church.

The divine service contains two things: sermons and singing. The sermons are limited almost entirely to morality and are only the better for it. The singing is in rather bad taste; and the French verses they sing are even worse. It is to be hoped that Geneva will reform herself on these two points. An organ has just been put in the cathedral, and

perhaps they will progress to the point of praising God in better language and with better music. Otherwise, the truth obliges us to say
that the Supreme Being is honored in Geneva with a propriety and
calm correctness not to be found in our churches.

We will perhaps not give such long articles to the vastest mon-
archies; but, in the eyes of the philosopher, the republic of the bees is
not less interesting than the history of great empires; it is perhaps only
in little states that one can find the model for a perfect political administration. If religion does not permit us to think that the Genevans have
effectively worked toward their happiness in the other world, reason
obliges us to believe that they are pretty nearly as happy as anyone can
be in this one:

O fortunatos nimium, sua si bona norint.[93]

Translator's Notes

1. "Heaven grant a better lot to the pious [or the good] and such madness to our enemies."

2. The French word which is translated throughout by *drama* is *comédie*, except where it means comedy in our narrow sense. *Comédie* originally meant any play with a happy ending, as opposed to tragedy; but very early it began to be applied to the whole of drama in French usage. The most common word for actor is *comédien*.

3. This expression (morals [manners]) is chosen to translate the French *moeurs*. Although the Latin *mores*, which is also used in English, is a perfectly adequate equivalent, it is not a word in common use and has been deformed by a certain technical use in contemporary sociology. The word *moeurs* is central to Rousseau's analysis of the theatre, and something of its sense must be maintained in translation in order for his teaching to have full weight. *Moeurs* are morals as they express themselves in the way of life or the customs of men and nations; they are akin to what we would call character. "Morals" in our usage tends to be too abstract, implying certain duties and rules which must be obeyed, while "manners" implies superficial politeness with little relation to the total meaning or value of a life. *Moeurs*, on the contrary, means habits as they are related to moral goodness or badness; a man's taste in food or where he goes to take his amusement indicate more adequately the state of his soul and the type of actions he is likely to take than any opinions or principles he holds; and the habits that appear in themselves to be of the most trivial or indifferent nature can play the most important role in the direction of the whole man. Hence, it is of the first importance to study the effect of any institution on the habits of men to understand its moral effect; from the legislator's point of view the *moeurs* are the source of a state's well- or ill-being and the decency or viciousness of its citizens. The moral and religious principles common in Paris and Geneva may well be similar, but the ways of life and the men who live them are utterly different, and, humanly speaking, this is what counts. As the least evil, *morals-manners* has been chosen to keep the reader aware of Rousseau's constant attention to the real practices of men in evaluating their moral worth; in spite of its inelegance as a translation, this expression serves to remind us both of the relation of habit to morality and the fact that morals express themselves in ap-

parently commonplace ways. Sometimes *moeurs* appears to mean either the one or the other exclusively, but the relation is always there.

4. Diderot. Rousseau thus announces publicly his break with his old friend.

5. "Though thou drawest a sword at thy friend, yet despair not; for there may be a returning. If thou hast opened thy mouth against thy friend, fear not; for there may be a reconciliation: except for upbraiding, or pride, or disclosing of secrets, or a treacherous wound: for these things every friend will depart."

6. Cf. Appendix, pp. 145–148.

7. Socinianism was a Christian sect closely allied with the development of Unitarianism. It took its name from its founder, Fausto Sozino, an Italian of the sixteenth century who lived in Poland for a long time, where his movement had great strength. It was popular throughout Europe and was accepted by many Protestant churches. Socinianism was anti-trinitarian and held that reason is the sole and final authority in the interpretation of the scripture. It further denied eternal punishments. Calvin had condemned the doctrine, so that the imputation in d'Alembert's article was both a daring interpretation of the doctrine of Geneva's pastors and one which was likely to be dangerous for them.

8. The parenthetical statement first appeared in the corrections to the first edition and disappeared in the edition of 1782.

9. Rousseau means *Instruction Chrétienne* (Geneva, 1752), by Jacob Vernet.

10. This declaration can be found in the appendices of both the Fontaine and Brunel editions.

11. David Hume.

12. The French word here translated by *theatre* is *spectacle* and has a much broader and richer meaning than the word *theatre* would imply. It is literally anything that one goes to see, and hence entertainment in general. Unfortunately, to translate *spectacle* in a more general way would render its specific sense of *theatre* unintelligible in English. But the reader should keep the other connotations in mind, for Rousseau does not limit himself to a discussion of the theatre narrowly conceived, but is investigating the moral effects and correctness of all the pleasures of the eyes and ears with particular reference to their most sophisticated form, the drama. For this purpose the French word is propitious in that its more specific meaning can always be broadened to include its generic sense, and hence the drama can be compared to other forms of entertainment. The very word *spectacle* recalls the general problem, while the word *theatre* does not. Most generally *spectacle* has been translated by *theatre*, but where impossible, *entertainment* has been used. *Spectacle* is the word used by Rousseau in the title of the work.

13. See note 9.

14. *Galanterie* is not an exact equivalent of gallantry as commonly used in English, where it today almost exclusively implies valor. The French implies attentiveness to ladies and can thus be a vice in Rousseau's view. The two usages have their common source in chivalry, when knights performed valorous deeds out of love for fair ladies. The French took the side of love and the English that of bravery in their development of the word. No satisfactory English equivalent can be found for the French, and, all in all, gal-

lantry makes the best translation. The word *galant*, translated as gallant, presents the same difficulty.

15. "Each led by his pleasures" (Virgil *Eclogues* II. 65).

16. A popular comedy in the eighteenth century representing a natural man, written by Delisle de la Drévetière.

17. Tacitus *Annals* XVI. 5; Suetonius *Vespasian* 4.

18. *Nanine*, or *Le Préjugé Vaincu*, by Voltaire.

19. Plutarch *Sulla* XXX.

20. Alexander (Plutarch *Pelopidas* 31).

21. Tacitus *Annals* XI. 2. (This passage was added later and appeared in the edition of 1782.)

22. *Reflexions critique sur la poesie et la peinture* (Paris, 1719), Part I, Section 3.

23. By Thomas Corneille.

24. Béat. Louis de Muralt, *Lettres sur les Anglais et sur les Français* (Zurich, 1725), Letter V, p. 375.

25. "For comedy aims at imitating men worse, and tragedy men better, than those of today" (*Poetics* 2).

26. *Catalina* and *Atrée* were written by Crebillon; *Mahomet* is by Voltaire.

27. Atreus.

28. Plutarch *Sayings of Unknown Spartans* 55.

29. The French word translated here and elsewhere by *audience* is *parterre*. Its exact English equivalent is *pit*, the word denoting the part of the theatre in which the poor paid low admission for the right to stand. It has, hence, a derogatory sense implying the tasteless mob, the *hoi polloi*.

30. "Censure is indulgent to crows, hard on pigeons" (Juvenal *Satires* II. 63).

31. *Le Bourgeois Gentilhomme.*

32. *Georges Dandin.*

33. *L'Avare.*

34. This sentence disappeared from the edition of 1782.

35. An imitation of a play by the same name of Calderon.

36. The audience liked the poem which Alceste ridiculed for Molière.

37. Immediately after the first edition, Rousseau substituted the following for the next lines: "It was they who first introduced those coarse ambiguities, no less proscribed by taste than decency, which were for a long time the amusement of evil-minded societies and the embarrassment of chaste persons, and of which the better tone, slow in its progress, has not yet purified certain provinces. Other authors, less shocking in their witticisms, let the former amuse fallen women and undertook to encourage cheats. Regnard, one of the more modest, is not the least dangerous. It is unbelievable, etc."

38. *Police* means that branch of government which has to do with public order and morality. Our narrower usage of the word is a strict result of a narrowed conception of the functions of government; for Rousseau, the word still maintains its broader significance.

39. This is a résumé of the last two acts of Regnard's *Le Légataire Universel.*

40. Constance is a character from Diderot's *le Fils naturel; Cénie* is a play by Mme. de Graffigny.

41. "Ignorant he of the treacherous breeze" (Horace *Odes* I. viii).

42. Virgil *Aeneid* V. 654.

43. Plutarch *Sayings of the Spartans: Euboedas and Areus* 1.

44. *L'hystoire et plaisante Cronique du petit Jehan de Saintré* was a novel by Antoine de la Salle written in the fifteenth century. It was adapted for the theatre, in the eighteenth century, by Gueullette.

45. "Unsightly is an old soldier" (Ovid *Amor.* I. ix. 4). (The passage continues, *turpe senex amor:* "unsightly is an old lover.")

46. Plutarch *Cato the Censor* 17; *Advice to Bride and Groom* 13.

47. "Against his will, against hers" (Suetonius *Titus* vii. 2). Rousseau adds, "against the spectator's will."

48. By Richardson.

49. *The London Merchant, or the History of George Barnwell,* by George Lillo.

50. Cf. p. 20.

51. Rousseau here plays upon the word *spectacle;* a moral theater would be "something to see" and would be a theatrical entertainment in itself.

52. Plutarch *On the Delays of the Divine Vengeance* 4, *Lives of Ogis and Cleamenes,* xxx, 3.

53. This tribunal was established by Louis XIV for the purpose of ending the practice of dueling. It did not succeed; Rousseau here criticizes it and shows how it ought to have been constituted.

54. A famous square in Paris where executions usually took place.

55. Cf. Saint Simon, *Memoires,* XIX, 174 (Chervel edition).

56. "If we may compare small things with great" (Virgil *Georgics* IV. 176).

57. The Consistory was composed of the pastors and twelve elders who exercised a general moral supervision over the city. The Chamber was appointed by the council for the purpose of guarding the sumptuary laws and also received the complaints of the consistory.

58. Anne Oldfield, 1683–1730, was the most famous English actress of her time.

59. Livy VII. 2.

60. *De Oratore* I. 61.

61. It is not in the *Pro Q. Roscio* that Cicero says this but in the *Pro Quintio,* ch. 25.

62. "Whoever appears on the stage, on the assertion of a praetor, is civilly dishonored." (Rousseau here quotes from memory, and the citation is not quite accurate although the sense is not altered. The actual quote is: *Infamia notatur . . . qui artis ludicrae pronuntiandive causa in scenam prodierit* [*Digesta* III. 2]).

63. *Atellanae* and *Exodia* were comic farces.

64. Rousseau's assertion that there was no theatre at Sparta is in error. M. Leroy of the Academy of Inscriptions wrote him to explain that there were the ruins of a theatre at Sparta, and he responded thanking Leroy in a letter dated November 4, 1758. Leroy's letter is in the edition of Geneva, 1782, Volume XXIII, p. 426.

65. Note added later and included in the edition of 1782.

66. Cf. note 24.

67. *Clarissa Harlowe*, by Richardson.

68. The word translated by *chasteness* in the following passage is *pudeur*, which means decent shame or bashfulness in relation to erotic matters.

69. Voltaire, *Discours en vers sur l'homme* (sixth discourse).

70. Plutarch *Sulla* 35.

71. Herodotus II. 35.

72. by Diderot. In the second *Entretien*.

73. A verse by Boileau from his *Satire X (sur les femmes)*.

74. Cf. Appendix, p. 141.

75. Cf. Appendix, pp. 142, 143.

76. This last sentence was added later by Rousseau and appears in the edition of 1782.

77. Herodotus III. 12.

78. The text in Livy has not been found.

79. The books go directly from the ladies who devour them to shopkeepers who use them to wrap their wares.

80. This last line was added later and appeared in the edition of 1782.

81. "Impostors": a play on the word: (1) cheats and frauds; (2) those who think up and impose taxes, perhaps tax-farmers.

82. "Then, it seems, if a man who is able by wisdom to take on all sorts of forms and to imitate all things should come to the city and wish to make a display of himself and his poems, we would get down on our knees in worship before him as one who is holy, wondrous, and sweet; but we would say that it is not lawful for such a man to arise in our city, and we would send him away pouring myrrh over his head and crowning him with wool; and we ourselves would make use of the more austere and less sweet poet and storyteller for our benefit, the one who would imitate the diction of the decent man and would speak the things which are said according to the patterns that we set down as law when we undertook to educate the soldiers." (Plato *Republic* 398a–b.)

83. "What harm does death do me? Virtue is strengthened by misfortune; It is destroyed by neither cross nor sword of a cruel tyrant."

84. The Escalade was an independence holiday at Geneva. Cf. Appendix, p. 141.

85. Daniel 5:5.

86. Comedy by Saint-Foix.

87. "Dedicate life to truth" (Juvenal *Satires* IV. 91). The context of this citation should be examined.

88. Plutarch *Sayings of the Spartans, Lycurgus* 12–14.

89. "Alas, hardly will the vine leaf defend the ripe grapes" (Virgil *Georgics* I. 448).

90. Plutarch *Spartan Institutions* 15.

91. Cf. Appendix, p. 148.

92. "About the little things the princes deliberate, about the big things everyone; yet even about the things which are in the power of the people to decide, the princes first consult" (Tacitus, *Germany*, 11).

93. "O fortunate and more than fortunate, if they only knew their own good."